STREET
SIGNS
CHICAGO

neighborhood and other illusions
of big-city life

Library of Congress Cataloging in Publication Data

Bowden, Charles.
    Street signs Chicago.

1. Chicago (Ill.)—Economic conditions.
2. Chicago (Ill.)—Social conditions.
3. Neighborhood. I. Kreinberg, Lew, 1936-
II. Younker, Richard. III. Title.
HC108.C4B66   307.7'6   81-38449
ISBN 0-914091-05-0   AACR2
ISBN 0-914091-06-9 (pbk.)

ISBN cl 0-914091-05-0
ISBN pa 0-914091-06-9

Book design by Siemens Communication Graphics.

Published by Chicago Review Press
            820 North Franklin
            Chicago, IL 60610

STREET
SIGNS
CHICAGO

**neighborhood and other illusions
of big-city life**

by Charles Bowden and Lew Kreinberg
photographs by Richard Younker
foreword by William Appleman Williams

Chicago Review Press   820 N. Franklin   Chicago, IL 60610

For Kathy
      CB

For Barbara—whose Raggedy Ann loves my Raggedy Andy.
      LK

Table of Contents

Acknowledgements

A lot of people have helped us. For support and encouragement, we must thank Marcia Brice, Bob Giloth, Bob Johnson, Nancy Lee, John McEvoy, Carolyn Moore, Debbie Morrow, Tom Sheridan, Steve Starr, William Appleman Williams, The Jewish Council on Urban Affairs, and The Community Renewal Society. Also, part of the work was done under a grant from the John Simon Guggenheim Memorial Foundation.

Carl Smith proved invaluable as our editor; we are grateful for his innumerable suggestions.

This book has gone through many drafts and forms and each successive effort was read and endured by Barbara Kreinberg and Kathleen Dannreuther. We thank them for their patience and tip our hats to their stamina.

A special debt is owed to Dr. Ben P., Vincent H. C., and Tunia S., who saw the book in its true perspective and never let the argument pussyfoot around.

Foreword

I have been learning important matters about America from Lew Kreinberg and Chuck Bowden ever since I met them: Lew has been giving me tutorials for twenty years; and Chuck's exceptional book, *Killing the Hidden Waters* (1977), was of great help to me in developing a course in comparative maritime cultures.

Bowden and Kreinberg have been friends, and colleagues on the faculty of the College of Asking the Right Questions, for many years; and this book will explain why I wish they had collaborated much earlier. Lew was always an inspired talker. He speaks sentences, paragraphs, and even whole essays, with a style and verve that he too seldom takes the time to transcribe onto paper. I suspect that Chuck is as good in a rap as he is with a pen; but in any event he infused his book on Water and the Papago Indians with a special power through his command and use of the language.

His food lacked salt. He sought vile herbs for seasoning. He did not smoke, he did not take snuff, he did not drink. He did not sleep in a bed. Two coarse shirts sufficed for a wardrobe, the sweat-blanket off his horse for the night. But then he slept very, very little. Prayer took up his space time, and when he prayed he wept.

That is master carpentry. The writer is at the level where the next step is building spiral staircases. And that, among other things you will learn in this book, is extremely difficult. Awesome. It is such a great art that we ordinary folk think about beautiful and well-formed women in deeply-cut gowns descending the steps rather than about the carpenter who built the staircase.

The art in this book is that we readers think about the people and the issues and our responsibilities rather than about the authors. I do not know which men wrote which sentences, paragraphs, sections, or chapters. I would lay a year's wages that it never entered their heads to keep count. We are the beneficiaries of their neighborhood and community.

II

But what is neighborhood, and what is community?

One way and another, in most of what I have written, I have repeatedly invoked the spirit of those human realities. I have often been criticized for being vague, if not nostalgic and irrelevant and romantic; and in response I have been frustrated by what has seemed to me to be a casual willingness—even a willful eagerness—to forget or deny something very real from our history that could help us in the present and the future.

Kreinberg and Bowden have taught me—and will teach you—something very important about all of that. That is the greatest value of their book: agree with them or not, they stimulate and engage our minds. They insist that we rethink our assumptions about the nature and practice of life in America.

Their basic proposition is that there never have been any neighborhoods in Chicago, and that the effort to think about the city's history and present condition in those terms is at best misguided and at worst a tool of manipulation used by the people who exercise centralized power.

They develop their argument along two lines, and through a marvelously evocative ebb and flow of individual vignettes and cameos and broad analyses that move back and forth through time. First, they suggest that Americans mistakenly talk about neighborhood in terms of the European village, a way of life which evolved through generations of people staying in the same place where they earned their living and built their culture. This never happened in the industrial cities of the United States, and certainly not in Chicago.

Second, they demonstrate that the geography which defined Chicago—the juncture of the Great Lakes and the Mississippi River system—doomed it to be a way station to some other place. It was from the outset a center for populating, exploiting, and dominating a vast hinterland. Thus no classic neighborhoods could develop: one largely ethnic group of people moved into a given area and then moved on to be followed by another wave of migrants.

But now, they continue, Chicago's hinterland has become populated and rationalized. Hence, its destiny fulfilled, the city becomes increasingly dysfunctional. Mayor Daley's "City That Works" is not working. In an eerie and chilling chapter, Bowden and Kreinberg illustrate this by describing the truly absurd efforts to solve the water problems of Chicago by drilling tunnels through the aquifers that provide drinking water in order to store surplus sewage. It is a civilian version of the irrational MX missile program.

And at the end, Kreinberg and Bowden point out that all large American cities—including the "new" ones in the Sunbelt—fact the same future unless we as a culture change our assumptions of unlimited growth and mobility.

III

So we are back to the issues of neighborhood and community. And here I wish the authors had widened the scope of their argument to include cities other than Chicago. They do review the brave efforts of Blacks to create in Lawndale a village in which people work and play and develop a multi-generational culture. But I wish they had done that in the context of London, England, and Melbourne, Australia.

Let me tell you what I mean. I was born and reared in an American equivalent of what Lew and Chuck refer to as a European kind of village. Atlantic, Iowa, grew to be a town of about 5,000 souls between 1876 and 1941. It was an important point for collecting the agricultural wealth that went east to Chicago, and for distributing the people, and the capital and consumer goods, that came west from Chicago.

But Atlantic also developed a great corn canning factory and a significant fertilizer industry. Hence it created and sustained an identity and character of its own which it retains to this day. Of course the village has changed since 1941, but it remains Atlantic, Iowa.

Here is where I suggest that Chuck and Lew might have driven home their argument more forcefully. London and Melbourne are surely as much the creatures of geography as Chicago. Furthermore, both of those large cities were the centers—the dominating metropolitan hubs—of *changing* hinterlands. Yet both developed as, and very largely remain defined as, *collections of villages.* That is the essence of their viability, their livability, even their charm.

Hence my point is not so much to challenge but to reinforce the Bowden-Kreinberg analysis. America *does* have a tradition of villages. Having lived in London and Melbourne, I like those cities *because* I was born and raised in a village. And I am even so bold as to suggest that America once had cities that, at least for a fleeting moment, were moving in that direction. I knew Chicago and New York as an 18-year-old—and got to know their villages. I walked free and safe as a kid from Iowa in Harlem and in South Side Chicago. It *can* be done.

Early in this book, Lew and Chuck comment on an effort to introduce "neighborhood technology" into Pilsen.

Nobody is quite sure what neighborhood technology means, but everybody senses it concerns matters too inconsequential for large groups of people to bother with.

Point well taken, and nicely made. So we begin to create villages based on such technology. And in doing so we create neighborhood and community. And, who knows, perhaps even cities on a human scale.

That can be dismissed as Utopian. To do so, however, is to dismiss America. For America is in trouble because it has settled for more of the same instead of imagining a new and more civilized Utopia.

William Appleman Williams
June 1981

tarts at Night

:k T-shirt shouted advice.
anna soar with the eagles
't stay up with the owls.

was fat, beer belly fat, and his forty years were
l over his body. He stood there in his levis under a
ead 2:30AM. Booze made him wobble, but then
e in the line was loaded too. The grill at the White
d with hamburgers and diced onions. The waiting
ped a few bites would douse the fire in their ali-
ls. Everyone was terrified at the thought of dawn.
lared with white walls and stainless steel surfaces,
lay case for the city of night. Two cops gabbed at
vallowed coffee to pull them through the grave-
e help yelled orders and the line bobbed and
rd the greasy shrine of the grill. A bunch of Latin
i. They saw the cops and stopped dead at the

"Hey, Wolf," one kid finally hollered, "how come you not on the West Side, man? What you doin' in my neighborhood?"

The cop came alive over his coffee.

"My name," he roared, "is all over these streets."

The fat guy with the black T-shirt came bumping down the line with his bag of burgers. He sliced through the kids at the door like an ore boat plowing down the Lake from Duluth. All the eyes in the place idly watched him escape with his treasure.

Outside in the parking lot they caught him hopping into a restored classic car. Exhaust pipes writhed out from under the

17

hood like silver snakes. For a dome light, he had a crystal chandelier. The seats caressed his big ass with soft leather. Sitting next to the guy was this blonde. She was the original big blonde, with a couple of buttons unbuttoned on her blouse and cleavage down to her toes. He turned the key and the engine crackled, popped and then purred. The whole joint watched as they slid off into the Chicago night.

The natural way to talk about cities is as anecdotes about people. Chicago is the Mother Lode of urban stories—Al Capone, Stacker of Wheat, Hog Butcher of the World, The Machine, and baseball teams that always fade in August. A man will tell you that he handed his passport to a customs officer in some bleak corner of Africa and had the guy spin on him grinning, "Chicago! Cheecago!—rat a tat rat a tat tat!".

But to understand cities it is also necessary to think of them as abstractions—economies, demographies and ecologies. Besides being the place people live, they are the place where resources concentrate and energy is devoured. Chicago is as much a product of the Mesabi Range as the product of the Machine, as much the home of hardwood forests as the home of Poles. If you dig deeply into the past of Chicago, you will find both Jane Addams and Illinois coal.

Chicago has been called the city of neighborhoods because people are easier to talk about than ore bodies and railroad tracks. But the name misleads. Neighborhoods have never been the point of Chicago or any other large city. The city has been about the Lake, the canal, the river, the railroads, the airport, mills, factories, banks. Neighborhoods have always been afterthoughts.

Many people today see Chicago as a city on the skids. It is useful here to look at the past. Even in its heyday Chicago found it impossible to provide clean air, clean water, safe streets, decent housing. Yet most efforts to fix the city hearken back to a time when it was said to work. Who did it work for?

Some claim that to revive Chicago, skyscrapers are just the tonic required. Others suggest leveling districts under the banner of urban renewal. Still others contend that the problem is people. They say boot out the poor and import the rich or at least the middle class. This swap is called gentrification.

None of these plans recognize that the rich resource base that built Chicago is diminished and that the price of doing business in the city has gone up. Nor do they recognize that even when things were cheaper Chicago did not do well by its citizens.

This book argues that Chicago's past is one of failure, and that Chicago's future is one where the cheap resources that made it boom will not exist. It operates from the assumption that the industrial city typified by Chicago in the late nineteenth and early twentieth century is finished, and it makes several claims:

The city of neighborhoods was never about neighborhoods.

The city that worked was a bad place to work.

The city of the future will be molded by declining resources and rising prices.

The city is not likely to die whatever the hardships ahead. The millions of people in America's urban centers have no place to go. We have become too numerous to return easily to the land.

Finally, we must remember the fat guy in the black T-shirt with the big blonde. Such dreams have always been what made the cities bearable. When the tail lights on his car disappeared into the wet Chicago night, he and the blonde had made dawn an easier thing to face.

1 Walks

The old man took long walks.

He'd leave the brick two-flat around 79th and Ashland and start marching on the center of Chicago. His path down Halsted snaked through the neighborhoods—Auburn, Gresham, Englewood, New City, Bridgeport, Lower West Side. The old man did not use these tags; hardly anybody did. Places were streets, numbers—79th and Ashland, or places were people. For him the walk went from Irish to blacks to Irish to Mexicans to Jews to Italians to Greeks to the Loop.

He loved the walk.

He'd say the city was going to hell, neighborhoods were sliding into ruin, parks turning into jungles.

He'd say the city used to be better, safer.

For dress, he preferred army surplus tennis shoes. He'd cut hunks out of the sides to air his feet. A stubble of beard splattered his face, an old cap snug on his head. His fingers on his right hand were stained from smokes; he rolled his own. Fat, he followed a beer belly everywhere he went. On his nose booze had made a map of fine red veins. His eyes were clear and sharp and on the alert as he walked.

He was a city man.

He loved the city, he hated the city. He'd finger the stolen goods on Maxwell Street, listen to the haggling. Maybe he'd buy a tamale from a Mexican vendor, watch the gypsies drum up a trade in the future. The fact that you could get anything in this town was an important fact for him. Get your hat from a Jew, lunch from a Kraut, clothes from the last war. His city was

21

where things got made. His city was where things happened. His city was where the people had gathered.

This was all part of the walks as he passed small factories, big factories, stood on the balcony in the Loop downtown and watched the orderly ferocity of the grain exchange. His treks took him past garden after garden as people struggled to raise memories in the sooty air and clay soil. Tomatoes at the start, then into a black belt of okra, snow peas among the Chinese, chilies in the Mexican stretch, ending in eggplant and plum tomatoes among the Italians and Greeks. All this in his city.

When it rained his basement flooded full of sewage. He'd sit on the steps watching the muck rise, then endure the stench as he hosed and swept it out. He didn't like that. He didn't like fixing traffic tickets when the cops pounced on him for speeding; he didn't like traffic. The politicians were crooked and city hall was full of deviltry. He shrugged it off. The neighbors got burgled, Christ! he never heard a thing and him sitting right there in the kitchen just ten feet from where they broke in. He remembered the look of the place with stuff scattered all around, the drawers all dumped out. Animals. He slept with a loaded .45 by his bed.

He remembered the Century of Progress exhibition in the thirties. He'd gone many times; hell, a hundred thousand people a day had gone. A green building, a purple building, a yellow building. What a spectacle. The pavilions, the lights, the future, boy, the future looked swell. That could only happen in Chicago.

So it wasn't so simple for the old man.

Things were possible here, he thought.

Things got made here.

In the end, he went off to the Sunbelt.

He'd say, I never said anything against Chicago. I always liked Chicago.

He read the Chicago papers every day.

Father Jacques Marquette and Louis Joliet hauled Chicago to the center of European thinking. It was the summer of 1673. They paddled from St. Ignace on the Strait of Mackinac the seventeenth of May. Two birch bark canoes floated seven men, smoked meat, dried corn, questions.

Did the Mississippi pour into the Gulf of Mexico or the Gulf of California or to some western sea?

Could France win North America by tracking this river?

Was China near?

The canoes were muscled by dreams of empire, furs and lost souls. Marquette dedicated the venture to an idea central to his Jesuit heart though not yet sanctioned by the Pope. He told his journal of the Immaculate Conception.

> The day of the Immaculate Conception of the Holy Virgin; whom I had continually invoked since I came to this country . . . to obtain from God the favor of being enabled to visit the nations on the river Mississippi. . . .

> Above all, I placed our voyage under the protection of the Holy Virgin Immaculate, promising that if she granted us the favor of discovering the great river, I would give it the name of Conception.

The French took the long way to Chicago. First, down Green Bay and into the land of the Menomonies. The tribesmen said that people on the Mississippi would kill the French, that the river sheltered a demon who roared loudly and swallowed men and canoes. Do not push on, the tribesmen begged. For if that happened, the Menomonie would cease to occupy the edge between Europe and America, and if they ceased to occupy the edge, then trade would leave their hands.

Marquette and Joliet paddled the Fox until it dwindled, then portaged the mile and one half to the Wisconsin. They had crossed over into the Mississippi watershed. On the seventeenth of June, the men glided onto the great river, "with a joy which I cannot express," reported Joliet. A giant catfish rammed the canoe. Buffalo grazed on the shore. Eight days downstream they found their first human footprint. Soon a succession of tribes entertained them and listened to their explanations of the true faith. All these people held European knives, European axes, European guns, iron and beads. They were part of the trade trail that was the Mississippi.

Near Alton, Illinois, monsters glared from the rocks. Red, black, green, "as large as a calf, with horns like a deer, red eyes, a beard like a tiger, and a frightful expression of countenance." recalled the French. "The Face is something like that of a man, the body covered with scales; and the tail so long that it passes entirely round the body, over the head, and between the legs, ending like that of a fish."

Manitou, the painted demons that people in that part of the country used to explain power to themselves. The French were frightened; they were far from the symbols of their God. Seven men in two birch bark canoes on a powerful river confronting the bold marks of demonic forces. They were strangers and they felt their weakness.

Mike's saloon hunkers at 16th and Halsted in Pilsen, once the city's Bohemian district. The Loop's about two miles northeast, the lake a mile to the east. He has hung a sign near the door:

La Raza
Mejicana
Espanol
Latino
Hispano
or
Chicano
or whatever you call me
I look the same
I feel the same
I cry the same.

Everybody in the place looks the same. Mexican. The housing in the neighborhood runs two to three stories, flats and apartment buildings. This Pilsen was originally named after the Bohemian town that gave the world a beer so fine it became a type. Stand in the bar doorway and the district looks run down. Here and there the steps need replacing, some porches sag. All the windows are in place but the garbage has trouble staying in the garbage cans. Yet out there is Mexico, just as decades ago out there was central Europe.

Between beers, Mike hands out mail to men who drop by. This saloon is an address. The building is a two flat, and next door is a big lot, fenced. Leaning against Mike's building, a greenhouse, thrown up by local people, the boys in the bar, and thought up by community organizers in the name of neighborhood technology. Nobody is quite sure what neighborhood technology means, but everybody senses it concerns matters too inconsequential for large groups of people to bother with. Neighborhood technology weighs in at about the size of the guys drinking beer at Mike's. Next to the green house stretch rows of chilies, tomatoes, tomatillos, bell peppers, beans, corn, and five little apple trees. The hunger of Emiliano Zapata for land has shown up at 16th and Halsted. Mike pours beer, delivers the mail, lends his land to the urban farmers, gets fat. He goes to hearings, he argues, he tries to figure it all out.

This is no easy task since the city has no memory and the past is erased daily. Everything happens again and again because everything happens for the first time. In 1886, workers went on strike in Chicago. They wanted an eight hour day. They got the Haymarket riot. The city memorializes this struggle with a statue to the police. Nobody remembers, so how are Mike and his patrons supposed to find out. The Bohemians are almost gone from the neighborhood, mainly you see old people gone to fat and heavy overcoats. A hundred years ago they worked in wood, were 1/40 of the city's population and most of its communists. Their memorial is the local church, Providence of God.

A mile or so from Mike's bar is the bulldozed site of the International Harvester reaper works, Cyrus McCormick's monument. While the guys at the bar fret over *La Migra* and puzzle out the English language, they drink blissfully ignorant of the fact that seventy years before men much like themselves, men who looked much the same, were handed brochures by the Harvester management to help them understand their place in things. Here's Lesson One for the Poles:

I hear the whistle. I must hurry.
I hear the five minute whistle.
It is time to go into the shop.
I take my check from the gate board and hang
it on the department board.
I change my clothes and get ready to work.

The starting whistle blows.
I eat my lunch.
It is forbidden to eat until then.
The whistle blows at five minutes of starting time.
I get ready to go to work.
I work until the whistle blows to quit.
I leave my place nice and clean.
I put all my clothes in the locker.
I must go home.

Apparently the schools fail. Nobody seems to remember these things. Not around here. Nobody speaks of these things. The guys at the bar get their mail, and laugh and talk. Mike puts up signs.

. . . whatever you call me
I look the same
I feel the same
I cry the same.

———————

Chicago, the city that worked. A din that taught Carl Sandburg tones and tempos, a smithy for American speech, a place by river and lake that really did butcher hogs for the world and beckon country boys with warm whores under the hissing gas lights. A city that could make anything and use anybody.

"Wer geht kein America?" asked the Jews. "Die snayders, shusters and fergaonovim." Who leaves for America? The tailors, shoemakers and horse thieves. In 1897, the Russian census counted 6,000 rabbis; twelve years later less than 350 had fled the pogroms for America.

"The contadino, the man from the country," a witness explained to Senator Dillingham's 1911 immigration hearings, "[is] a healthy animal, ignorant, but with splendid adaptability, quick to learn, bright, considering that he is a descendant of a race ill treated for centuries. . . . They are very rugged and strong. . . . They are capable of doing a day's work and possess a great deal of endurance. . . . ''

What did these people do? They wrote letters home confessing that in America a man must do the work of three horses. Here is the first day in the steel mill for an Austrian Jew:

> The man put me in a section where there was terrible noises, shooting, thundering and lightning. I wanted to run away but there was a big train in front of me. I looked up and a big train carrying a big vessel with fire was making towards me. I stood numb, afraid to move, until a man came to me and led me out of the mill.

One immigrant worker concluded, "A good job, save money, work all time, go home, sleep, no spend."

This world has ended and the city that worked is increasingly the city that counts. The jobs which beckoned healthy animals have disappeared into machines or left town for lower taxes, cheaper wages, more sunshine. The economists cover this fact with columns of numbers that prove more things are being made, more people are consuming more things. Everybody's better off than their grandfather.

But grandfather is dead. For the living, the facts are that the jobs take more skills, that the people working expect more from the jobs than simple survival. The hell with the statistics tumbling from the mayor's office. If you are poor and dark and do not speak English, if you are ignorant and have little to offer but strength and grit, you are in trouble. The guys at the bar in Mike's will take anything and just manage. Their children will demand more and will join the city's warrens of unemployed and underemployed.

Once factories advertised for hands and they meant just that.

Hands. Backs. Arms. Legs. Animals. Deep inside the city where the blacks and Latins and young males loiter, that fabled first rung of the economic ladder is getting harder to grasp. Paradise slips away. We all know this. We say progress, believe progress, we've got the numbers to prove progress. Then we look outside the car window, glance up from the newspaper as the train roars us to work, and we see and we know all over again.

Yet the people keep coming, following some yellow brick road laid down by the Jews, or was it the Italians? Those communist Bohemians? Greeks? Lithuanians? Estonians? Letts? Poles?

Something keeps them coming and coming. Whatever lurks back there in Mississippi and Michoacan pushes people toward us.

The French sped down the river. Toward the end of June, they floated in peace, their talk full of the demons they had seen painted on the rocks. Then, "we heard the noise of a rapid, into which we were about to run. I have seen nothing more dreadful. An accumulation of large and entire trees, branches, and floating islands was issuing from the mouth . . . with such impetuosity that we could not without great danger risk passing through it. So great was the agitation that the water was very muddy and could not become clear."

They had found the mouth of the Missouri.

The men pushed on, crossing the mouth of the Ohio, down the great river until 700 miles above New Orleans they stopped. To go further would mean Spanish dungeons. There was no more to learn in that direction. The river they had entered from the Wisconsin was the same waterway that gushed into the Gulf of Mexico. They had found the geographic key to the center of the continent.

On the way upriver they went to Chicago. Up the Illinois through prairie and wood rife with buffalo, elk, deer, wildcats, geese, swans, ducks, parroquets and beaver. The land was laid out like a banquet table. The French saw through the wilderness to the food factory inherent in its abundance. One last thing remained unseen. A link was needed between the natural riches of the midcontinent and the commercial appetites of Louis XIV's Versailles. The native Americans showed the Europeans the way.

A simple paddle up the Des Plaines, an easy portage across a bog, then the Great Lake, Michigan. Joliet was struck by the feeble land wall between the two drainages. He suggested a canal be dug.

The French had found all the pieces that made Chicago possible. A rich heartland drained by great rivers. Adjacent, the Great Lakes, the largest jugs of fresh water on the planet and a gateway to the ocean and Europe. Between the two water systems, a bog, low ground on the edge of things. Here converged the sea lanes of the earth.

A place called Chi-ca-gou by the local people.

Mike the bartender and his Mexican friends are seen as the newest wrecking crew to have at the city. It is a wonder that after waves of Germans, Irish, Swedes, Bohemians, Poles, Jews, Italians, Greeks, Blacks and what not, there is any city left to pummel. But everyone says there is.

For the Mexicans the sense of destruction is often self destruction. In the 1920s Mexican steel workers liked this song:

I came under contract from Lorelia
To earn dollars was my dream
I bought shoes and I bought a hat
And even put on trousers.
For they told me that here the dollars
Were scattered about in heaps
That there were girls and theaters
And that here everything was fun.
And now I'm overwhelmed—
I am a shoemaker by trade
But here they say I'm a camel
And good only for pick and shovel.
What good is it to know my trade
If there are manufacturers by the score
And while I make two little shoes
They turn out more than a million?
Many Mexicans don't care to speak
The language their mothers taught them
And go about saying they are Spanish
And denying their country's flag . . .
My kids speak perfect English
And have no use for Spanish,
They call me 'fadder' and don't work
And are crazy about the Charleston.
I am tired of all this nonsense.
I am going back to Michoacan.

But many don't, and for those that stay in Pilsen, a constant worry is not just the poverty or bad housing or immigration officials or police shakedowns or loss of language. The thing feared is new housing entering the area under the cover of urban renewal. A fixed up Pilsen will have no room for Mexicans who are trying to fix themselves up.

A mile or so away, a contraption of condominiums and townhouses called Dearborn Park is rising on the vacant railroad land south of the Loop. *Chicago Magazine* hosts a bright, full page color advertisement: "THE GRAND OPENING OF CHICAGO'S NEXT GREAT NEIGHBORHOOD." Want to move into the neighborhood? Plunk down $40,000 to $140,000. The artwork shows green lawns and plump Grant Wood trees. Dearborn Park, the ad reassures, will have its very own public school. So relax.

Dearborn Park is urban renewal. No bodegas.

Urban renewal does not mean renewing people or renewing buildings. It means replacing poor people with middle class people and rich people. From the President on down, when politicians talk of renewing the city they mean eviction. The society can only conceive of fixing up neighborhoods by leveling them and driving the people off.

Close attention must be paid to words like neighborhood and renewal because they can kill. The politicians and community leaders who speak highly of renewing places also like to describe neighborhoods as the fundamental units of American cities. Chicago, for example, describes itself as the city of neighborhoods. This is not true.

Chicago is a city of factories, railroads converging on the bog, bankers counting the take, steel, gadgets, profit and loss. Neighborhoods come so far down this list that they are off the page. Nobody came to Chicago to found a neighborhood or to save the lake shore for swell parks. Nobody came for the weather. People talk of neighborhoods because they offer a sense of personal boundaries in the miles of city.

But the neighborhoods, the old neighborhoods, are not the tail that wags the dog. They are just located on the ass end of this dog.

Cities are not about neighborhoods.

The city that worked is losing the work.

Two things to remember.

But things are so easy to forget in the city. Pilsen is a case in point. The boys in Mike's bar, the people in the street see things like Dearborn Park rising nearby, and on reflection they can puzzle out what it will mean for them. But most of the time no one reflects. The day is filled with making a living, catching the bus. A place like Pilsen slumbers on only half awake to what is happening around it, only half aware of what has happened to it before.

This place has a past of sweat and blood. "Hoodlum" came into the American language to describe nineteenth century adolescents from streets like Pilsen's. Right here, men thought up ideas like the eight hour day, and the general strike that would still machines from coast to coast. Just outside Mike's saloon at 16th and Halsted, there in the underpass of the Burlington and Chicago and Alton tracks, Pilsen entered the history books in July of 1877.

Americans had stopped the locomotives running across the northern tiers of states. At first the issue was wages, then the eight hour day. Finally, questions arose about the thing itself, capitalism. Chicago was a strike center.

The army was called back from Indian wars on the plains; the local police swore in special deputies. The streets were full of working men, the factories silent and empty shells. The city began to divide into two camps. Those who worked in factories fell into one group. Those who owned factories, or businesses, or clerked in them or served in the police or Army were in the other group. The mayor asked the Board of Trade for volunteers; they sent twelve warriors, five being conscripted messenger boys. This movie was directed by Karl, not Groucho.

The two groups fought battles in the commercial and industrial districts. "The sound of clubs falling on skulls was sickening for the first minute," confessed the *Times,* "until one grew accustomed to it."

Toward the evening of July 25th, a shower washed the city. At six o'clock hundreds of men gathered at 16th and Halsted to shut down the Burlington railroad. Railroad strikers, lumberyard men, idle hands, young toughs, all swarming over the switchyard making certain that no rolling stock rolled. Just as the crowd was breaking up and drifting off, 18 policemen arrived. Rocks were thrown, the cops pulled their revolvers. A hundred shots were fired, hitting four men in the crowd.

Halsted was jammed with workers and wagons. They inched the police backward, then pushed them into a running retreat. They stoned railroad buildings, they bombarded an incoming passenger train. Windows fell to the sidewalk, and the men sacked two hardware stores and a gun store. A railroad worker dropped dead from a stray slug. Nine men lay wounded on the tracks. Night fell.

The Battle of the Viaduct. Right there, outside Mike's saloon at 16th and Halsted. This is not a story told at the Mexican bars or in any other bars.

The city forgets.

That makes three things to remember.

The people trickling back to the city and stimulating the renewal dollars forget also. They are middle class and upper middle class and they forget that the slums that must now be cleared were the neighborhoods that housed their ancestors. They do not remember poor ancestors.

Yet they are like the poor except they have more money. They want better schools, cleaner air. Good God, rid the river of that stench, plant some trees. Provide decent parking for Volvos. Because they have money, they can get these things, or some of these things. In a society devoted to consuming goods, they consume. They are what everything in the society points to. They are the ideal.

They require more steel, more lumber, more glass, more natural gas, more petroleum, more hot air in winter, more cool air in summer. More space. This is the good life. But they want more, everyone wants more, in a future that will provide less. Less energy, less lumber, less hot air in winter, less cool air in summer. Less everything that people consume. The glass towers that are cloning in the bankers' boardrooms require a tomorrow that will be like yesterday. So do the freeways, the giant office buildings.

They are all wrong answers to tomorrow.

We are redesigning the city for a set of appetites that are doomed. This standard of living is behind us, this way of living is ending. The big buildings are headstones, not touchstones. When the city bulldozes old houses for new apartment buildings, it destroys the possibly useful for the obviously useless.

The Chicago skyline was not built on new oil prices.

The skyline is terminal.

The city being plowed under, the old nineteenth century pre-petroleum city, might have possibilities. The city going up does not.

We are redesigning a city for a set of appetites that are doomed.

The final thing to remember.

Father Marquette returned to Chicago. Just as Joliet had seen the importance of a canal linking Lake Michigan to the Mississippi watershed, Marquette saw the spot as a junction between the Great Lakes and legions of souls in the center of the continent. Chicago was a place where things converged, whether native tribes, or the pelts of beavers.

A year had passed since the first voyage; November winds whipped the lake with storms. Marquette camped a few miles inland. French fur trappers worked the nearby countryside. The priest fell ill. His two French companions put up a hut. Marquette lay there as the storms of fall blew past. His mission to the nearby tribes was named the Immaculate Conception. He would win them to Christ. But first he must survive. Some Indians provided food; the French trappers looked in on the small party. The priest and his companions held a nine day novena seeking the intervention of the Virgin.

Marquette rallied.

The group portaged to the Des Plaines. The priest talked to a large gathering of Indians. He had brought four large paintings with him that illustrated key points of the faith. Then back to Chicago, a portage to the lake, and the journey home.

Marquette died in passage near what is now Ludington, Michigan.

The beer comes in two flavors, Schlitz or Old Style. If it's Mexican beer you need, a hit of Carta Blanca or one more taste of Dos Equis, well, best be off for old Mexico.

Mike, why don't you serve Mexican beer?

We got Schlitz and we got Old Style.

The light is dim in the bar, but it is not dark. The place feels good. The ceiling is old tin plate, the back bar a mountain of mahogany, nicely carved. A small decal on the wood advertises a beer not brewed for decades. Every couple of months some stranger drops by and a light bulb goes on in his head. He has found the diamond in the rough; he makes an offer for the back bar. Not for sale.

The decor is brief but varied. Two deer heads, a print with the look of an Aztec mural, a painting of two frigates crossing green water under blue skies, beer signs. In the back a pool table with the crack of balls slicing into the conversations at the bar.

In late afternoon, the place fills with men drifting home from work. They've got sacks of groceries under their arms. They have a beer or two, watch the pool games. No serious drinking. One stool is claimed by an old Bohemian. He was born around the corner and he's been coming here for a long time. He still has some teeth and nods and grunts through the salsa din of the saloon.

The place is more for agreeing than arguing, more for nods than sentences. Conversations in English and Spanish sound like lyrics in rock songs, clearly there but barely intelligible. A Mexican mechanic scurries in from his garage next door; he's back of the bar getting buckets of water, he has no water connection. He jokes with the guys at the bar. The work day is ending and everyone wants a beer. There is no anger. There are no women.

Mike is a big man. When he was younger they called him Tarzan. He has dark eyes and he kind of squints them so that he seems to be boring into things. His expressions change swiftly. For all his weight, he is intense and quick with his moves. He is

saying that he's good for a $100,000 mortgage out in the
suburbs but when he tries to get $40,000 for a scheme in Pilsen,
the banks laugh in his face. He has been saying this for years to
anyone who will listen.

Mike is a foot soldier in the urban renewal wars.

My name is Miguel X. I have twice lost my home due to
urban renewal. I live in the Pilsen area of Chicago. Again,
I am threatened by big business and city plans. The homes
in Pilsen are among the oldest in the city. Only ten percent
are owned by residents of the area. The vast majority are in
need of complete rehabilitation.

The people of my neighborhood are poor people. They
rank sixth from the bottom in income of Chicago's eighty-
six neighborhoods. The people in my neighborhood who
own homes cannot get loans to rehab their buildings. The
people who want to buy homes there cannot get the money
to buy their homes. My neighborhood is redlined by banks,
insurance companies and savings and loan associations.

This is the Catch 22 of city life and everyone knows it. If your
neighborhood is bad enough to need fixing, it cannot be fixed
because it is too bad to risk money on. Unless it is so bad that a
better class of people are attracted by the dirt cheap housing or
it gets so bad that it can be bulldozed. Then the ruins will bring
forth the bankers.

This reality, like the poor and the Chicago building code, has
been with us forever.

Racist inspectors come into my neighborhood who don't
speak Spanish. They harass and confuse the people who
can't even understand what they are talking about.

A man lives in Glencoe, Oak Park, Skokie, can own a
building in Pilsen for twenty years and never be bothered
by inspectors; but when one of my people scrapes all his

savings together and buys that same building, he will be told he will have to change the wiring, change the plumbing and put up new walls or else his building will be demolished.

I wish the officials and the presidents of some of these banks and insurance companies would come into our homes and see how my people must live. It's winter now. Many of the homes are cold. The lights in the hallways are frequently out. Rats enter and leave freely through large holes in the walls. Falling ceilings are injuring people.

What is one to make of this? Faced with poor people living in poor neighborhoods, the city suggests urban renewal. This means the poor will be booted out of their houses and that middle class people will move in and fix up the houses. Or the poor will be booted out of their houses and the houses bulldozed and new buildings thrown up before the middle class moves in. This is the solution put forth by politicians, bankers, professors, chambers of commerce. This is our best answer to these people and these places.

Everyone in the bar is laughing, having a good time. Next door, the garden promises tomatoes, chilies, beans. The greenhouse is almost done. Things will grow this winter.

From the doorway you can look past the tracks, look over the viaduct, and see Sears Tower, the world's tallest building, stabbing up from the earth two miles away.

Old Style, please.

———————————

Drink too much beer in the night, pour on the black coffee in the dawn and still it comes back down to one thing. Look behind all the categories, the glass towers, the slums, the old neighborhood, the mainline, the redline, the bad wires, broken pipes, inspect, inspect, and there it is, the power. Peel back the labels of city, peel back community, urban renewal, peel back neighborhood, and then you will find the power to make and break buildings, lakes, rivers and people.

Power moves in currents above and beyond places called neighborhood; power moves in money sliding down LaSalle Street to the Chicago Board of Trade, cruises around in limousines waving real estate plans, flashes by in electric lines nourished by nuclear fires, explodes in metal cylinders that drive automobiles, trucks, boats.

Power makes things happen. Neighborhoods have things happen to them. Big banks don't belong to neighborhoods. Skyscrapers don't belong to neighborhoods. Power plants don't belong to neighborhoods. The forces that determine cities like Chicago don't belong to neighborhoods.

People belong to neighborhoods, because they can't find much else to belong to. Neighborhoods are occasions, places where people hang their hats until they get the chance to move on. They lack the persistence, the organization and the strategy of the groups that exercise power. That's why they lose.

No magic here, no smoke, no mirrors, no rabbits, no hats. Can't drink enough beer at night, swallow enough black coffee at dawn. Remember something simple when the politicians, the real estate brokers and city planners start talking about the renewed city, the fixed-up city, the model city, the way the city will be if you give them their head. They've never built a city for people. When they start that talk about community, watch out.

Put your hand on your wallet.

Dead bolt that door.

Years after Marquette's death, they came off the lake mist, a band of friendly Indians toting a sack of dry bones. The priest's remains were interred by the Canadian Jesuits.

How much of his work lived on in this land?

From the very beginning the French goals were split between saving souls and harvesting furs. While Marquette prayed to the Virgin and explained the faith to tribes of Americans, Joliet noticed the abundance of the land and dreamed of the canal at Chicago linking the ocean to the center of the continent. But both goals fed off the location. The geographic power of Chicago was inherent whether one worshipped God or Mammon.

This convergence of waterways that gave the spot value overwhelmed the successive schemes. Fur trading overwhelmed missionary work, the village supplanted the trader's fort, the canal boat ended the village, the steam locomotive outstripped the canal, the highway took freight from the railroad, the freeways battered out yet another design for the city.

Chicago is the place where topography gathered things, whether at the river or at O'Hare. This is the fact Marquette and Joliet in their different ways understood. This is the point people today seem to forget. They find Chicago bewildering or plannable or reformable or a has-been or bankable. They forget it is geography, for decades, centuries, millenia.

Geography.

Geography in Mike's bar, geography in Sears Tower.

Geography does not explain everything, but without it very little can be explained at all, for Marquette or for ourselves.

Mike's been around Pilsen a long time, but he married an Irish woman from nearby Bridgeport, Mayor Daley's neighborhood. Here too geography mattered. He couldn't find a priest who would marry an Irish woman to a Mexican. So they had to leave her parish for the ceremony. This rankled him for years.

He bought a dog, an Irish Wolfhound, the largest kind of dog in the world. Mike had to send off to Europe for one. The dog turned into a prize winner; Mike still has a picture of the beast. He showed him off all over the country, even took him back to Texas for shows.

He had the only Irish Wolfhound in the area. Every year in Bridgeport they had a parade on St. Patrick's day. They'd come around and have to ask Mike to let the dog in the parade, his dog being the only Wolfhound available. Mike said sure. And so his daughter marched in the parade with the dog, the beast wearing a sign.

THIS DOG EATS BEANS.

Let's go through it all again.

The city of neighborhoods is not about neighborhoods.

The city that worked is losing the work.

The city with the past forgets its past.

The city being redesigned complements a future that is doomed.

This book looks into these points, past, present and future.

Its pages are stuffed with questions. Did Chicago ever really work for the men, women and children who lived in it? Can its growth and problems be understood without a close look at the flow of resources through its commercial arteries? In an era where cheap abundant resources decline, what lies in store for the older industrial cities as well as for the newer sunbelt boom-towns?

Many people think the American city has been largely a success story with a few small problems, like slums, pollution, traffic jams, things easily remedied with a bit of planning and study. Neighborhood a shambles? Renew it. Road crowded with cars and trucks? Freeways. Air dirty? We'll get to that, but give us some time. Sewage backup? We have a plan, it will take a few billion and some work, but no problem. Crime? Police. Shootings? We're gonna register guns. Rents too high? The Mayor's looking into it. Condos taking over? A task force. Jobs? Got a program.

Yes indeed.

Don't let the straight streets fool you.

There was another thing the old man used to do besides tramp across Chicago. He'd get on the El and ride down to the Art Institute. Hardly anyone else bothered from around 79th and Ashland. The thing fit, but it wasn't a simple fit. The train kept the old man and the Art Institute and where he lived, all in their proper places.

He'd look out the El window at the backs of flats and apartment buildings, not listening to the scream of the train on the rails. All the porches climbed the buildings wearing the same color of gray; all the lines of flapping clothes snapped in the sooty air. Some of the windows would be bricked up, but nobody really believed in the bricks. Inside, you knew the people could still hear those trains. They got used to it. Everybody said so. The trains seemed to vanish from their lives, get invisible. You'd be sitting there isolated in the noise of the train with the city flashing by the window, and suddenly you'd see a woman out on her porch just the other side of the glass hanging up the laundry wearing nothing but a bra and panties.

He'd get off at Washington and walk over to the Institute. He had no time for the lions outside, or the Van Goghs or Picassos or El Grecos. Bunch of daubs, that's not what things look like. He only had time for two things. One a painting of lions by Delacroix. Look at those eyes—the blue bites right off the canvas.

The other a Hopper, a night scene in a corner diner. You're looking through the big plate glass window into the harsh light of the diner. A couple of people, all so lonely. In the cold black of the city outside, the diner's cool electric fire is the only warmth to be had. He'd look.

Then he'd go home.

2 Them

September 5, 1976

Dear Son,

I sent you this letter hoping that you find yourself healthy in body and soul. Our situation since you left us is a little wearisome. We are not well. For the last few days we have been a bit sick.

The letter was stuffed in a shoebox with other scraps of a life in an abandoned building on 18th Street, neighborhood of Pilsen, city of Chicago. The place had been torched. Not much left but the charred hulk and little bits and pieces of someone.

THE SALVATION ARMY SETTLEMENT

Victory 2 5566   3053 S. Normal Avenue
Chicago, Illinois 60616

Date / 3-18-71

Quantity /	Description	Price / Amount
	Day Care Fee	20.00
THANK YOU		Total 20.00

UNION MEDICAL CENTER
serving Beef Boners and
Sausage Makers Union Local 100

YOUR UNION MEDICAL CENTER
WHAT MEDICAL SERVICES ARE PROVIDED?
HURT AT WORK? BEEN IN AN ACCIDENT?
WHO CAN USE THIS CENTER?
APPOINTMENTS MUST BE KEPT AND AT TIMES
SPECIFIED . . . .

We wanted to take your father to the doctor but were unable to because of lack of food for the animals. Sometimes he gets up early and sometimes late. Now he is feeling very tired.

Son, we received the money that you sent us with the boy from Tachiso—the one from Guapango—and for that we give you our most infinite thanks. The money is going to help us very much and we truly need it.

UNIVERSITY OF ILLINOIS HOSPITAL
Patient Accounts

Date/ 11-10-75
Patient Name   Raphael X.
Admission Date   10-6-75
Amount Owed   393.88

You have not paid this bill for the hospital charges.
Please pay the full amount within (10) days.
It is the policy to send unpaid bills to collection agencies.

Collection Correspondent

UNIVERSITY OF ILLINOIS HOSPITAL
Patient Accounts

To: Raphael X.
Date/ 1-15-76

Your payment of $200.00 on your hospital bill was received.
Thank you.
However, you still owe a balance of $244.23. May we have the balance as soon as possible.

Collection Correspondent

Son, I am going to recommend something that I believe is very good for you. Take care, son, to behave yourself. Remember that we all have a soul to save and that one not-too-distant day we are going to see ourselves before God. That is when we are going to repent but by then it is already late, very late, my son. Although I do not see you, I still feel a presentiment when something happens. Therefore I urge you to behave yourself while we are living far away from each other and send us a good remembrance of you. There are always diversions, son—good friends or bad ones—but you only have one set of parents. When God remembers us we will return to see you forever and ever.

THE DROVERS NATIONAL BANK OF CHICAGO
From: Raphael X.
To: Epigminia Vega X.
$416.42

G & A COMPANY, CHICAGO, ILLINOIS
Earnings Statement

Name: Raphael X.

Rate / Hours / Earnings			Type / Fed. With. Tax / FICA		
5.6550	37	209.24	Reg	42.88	29.43
8.4825	10	84.83	O/T		

State / GROSS / Net Pay / Period Ending			
6.81	295.32	243.87	1-02-76

You know that people talk about things that you don't know what to make of. Children's problems no matter how small cannot be ignored by their parents. For this reason I urge you to deport yourself well and follow a good road. It is not necessary to be great or small in order to be good, young or old to take advice. If you do not know yourself, ask someone who gives you good advice and follow what that person tells you to do. Finally, there are many good diversions like television and other things, very healthy without injuries of any sort. Behave yourself for that which you most want in life and always remember our Lord, commending yourself to him when you wake up. Ask him to guide you along the road to the Sacred Heart and the Blessed Virgin that they like us do not forget you. Ask this of them with fervor and we will also do the same for you.

**BEEF BONERS & SAUSAGE MAKERS UNION,
LOCAL 100**
1649 West Adams Street
Chicago, Illinois 60612
Phone 942-0555

Walter F. Piotrowski / secretary treasurer

Dear Member:
Welcome to Local 100 Beef Boners and Sausage Makers Union, AFL-CIO. The enclosed material explains the many benefits that are available to you and your family as a member of Local 100.

EL CAMINO DE LA VIDA ETERNA EXPLICADO

El Mundo—"Siglo Malo." Gal. 1: 4; "Puesto en maldad." 1 Juan 5: 19; "Se pasa."

SATANAS—"Principe de la potestad del aire." Efes. 2: 2.

PECADO—"Es Maldad." 1 Juan 5: 17

MUERTE—"Resulta de pecado." Sant. 1: 15.

JUICIO—"La hora de juicio esta determinada ya." Apoc. 14: 7.

CASTIGO ETERNO—"Iran estos al tormento eterno." Mateo 25: 46.

RAFFLE

Benefit for the Atlantic Players
1st Prize 17" color t.v.
2nd Prize Alarm clock radio
DRAWING DATE NOVEMBER 26, 1976
donation one dollar, winner need not be present.
1ER PREMIO UNA TV. A COLORES DE 17"
2DO PREMIO UN RADIO DESPERTADOR
No. 543

Son, if this letter reaches you please answer it when time and goodwill permit you to do so. With few or many words I will be content with whatever you wish to do. Let us know how you are and when you will find yourself here.

want to take any more of your time, son. Return to
or your rest and remember it is never too late to start

n't torture yourself by thinking too much. Think of
eat, rest and enjoy yourself, but do so healthily
y sort of detriment or injury.
ch your parents are saying to and wishing for you.

Vega X.
exico

RIFA DE CARRO
BUICK ELECTRA 225 1969 (FULL POWER)
de Acuerdo Latoria Na. de Mexico
del dia 22 de Octubre, 1975
Ramon Briseno   1166 W. Armitage
Valor $20.00
No. 083

STEPHENS PHARMACY
1891 S. Throop Street

No. _____ Raphael X.
Una capsula 2 veces al dia. 5-28-75. LIBRAX #30

3 Dead Reckoning

Talk of the shotgun came after the meeting in the basement of Providence of God Church. The gathering was with the alderman everyone thought was syndicate. The residents of Pilsen were making one of their periodic efforts to control this thing everyone said they were: a neighborhood.

They had come together because they feared that someone might fix up an abandoned brewery a few blocks from the church. They feared that the pile of bricks would meta-morphose into studios and apartments for artists. A cafe with French bread and queer cheeses might pop up next to a bodega, or, God forbid, a fern bar. Rumor had it that the brewery was destined to be something called a mixed media center. For the people waiting in the basement that evening for their meeting to begin, quality was a crucial issue. By and large they wanted nothing to do with quality. Anything nice would cost more than people living in the area could afford to pay. Pilsen shouted a steady thunder of statistics: about 85% Mexican, maybe 6,000 illegals, 20% unemployment, 70% high school drop out rate, housing shrinking at about 100 units per year with the buildings being either bulldozed or burned.

The locals had learned to be wary of schemes to fix places up. From a single house middle class standards might spread like a plague, leaving pottery dangling from macrame in every window, oak floors sanded, polished and trapped under a shield of polyurethane, blocked fireplaces restored to firewood, flush toilets flushing, old walls bleached to stark, decorator white, and cuisinarts skulking on the drainboard.

55

This was one terror.

The other was jobs.

Mixed media centers were not notorious for employing masses of Mexicans. "The economic backbone of a community is not just a jeans store or a pizza shop," argued a worried local factory owner. He was also concerned that the local artists pushing for the brewery as a fine arts fortress were a bit soft in the head. "I saw one last year," he remembered with disbelief, "trying to plant a garden between ties on the railroad tracks. Trains still use those tracks."

The people of Pilsen, mainly Mexicans with a few pockets of old Bohemians and a few clumps of artists, paid cheap rent. This was the common thing that held together the neighborhood. Mostly, they lived in old dumps, which when tossed up a century ago were new dumps. This bend of the Chicago River had never been a Gold Coast. It had always been a port of entry for immigrants, a slum.

The local people and the alderman down in the basement of the Catholic church had to deal with these facts of cheap housing and fixing up an old brewery and one more thing. They all had to tussle with the idea of neighborhood. Outside the door all those ugly statistics slapped everyone in the face. But in the crowded smoky atmosphere of the meeting these same facts of unemployment, bad housing and powerlessness grew indistinct whenever anyone invoked the neighborhood. Suddenly, once the word was uttered the crowd was a community, an organic whole bravely working together for a better future. And so the crowd, the alderman, and a visiting expert from the city planning department began a vague kind of debate which at moments would heat up and then suddenly become witless as the myth of the good old neighborhood obscured their vision and scrambled up their minds.

The old settlers of these earlier immigrant races used to tell about how they were 'pushed out of the section by Jews.' The Bohemians said they had been 'forced' to leave one colony after another by Jewish invasion of their province. First they were on Franklin Street east of the River, then on Harrison Street, then on Twelfth Street (Roosevelt Road), until a Jewish group of newer immigrants seemed to come crowding into every available space. . . .

—Edith Abbott, *The Tenements of Chicago,* 1931

Pilsen curved along the river on the east and south. The northern border was the railroad tracks at Sixteenth Street across from Mike's saloon. To the west, the frontier was Western Avenue where Cyrus McCormick built his reaper works. These lines were set down by sociologists at the University of Chicago in the twenties who felt that science could not tackle the city until it was chopped up into units that would submit to census and theory. Now these designations live on oblivious to the city they label, and the residents of Pilsen argue their case under the banner of a Bohemian town, though they speak the name with a Spanish accent and send their kids off to the new local high school, Benito Juarez. The neighborhood lines and names linger on as monuments to a social science that never became a science.

At the meeting the neighborhood of Pilsen broke into three basic groups. First, the old Bohemians were there, sitting in rows like fat sacks left over from the Depression. The men wore caps, the women were encased in the armor of old coats. Before the show got underway, they huddled around the alderman, bitching and moaning about garbage pickup and whatnot. A major recreation in the city that works is listing the several hundred thousand items that do not work.

One old man lamented how when the Dan Ryan Expressway snaked past his house in the fifties they—those people who build superhighways—tore up the sidewalks. They said they'd fix them. Well, they never did. Now he lives in his old house with the truck traffic of the mid continent whizzing through his dreams and the sidewalk's all busted up.

What about my sidewalk?

But the slum conditions remain. The remedy is the same as has been resorted to world over: first, the cutting of broad thoroughfares through the unwholesome districts; and secondly, the establishment and remorseless enforcement of sanitary regulations which shall insure adequate air-space for the dwellers in crowded areas, and absolute cleanliness in the street, on the sidewalks, and even within the buildings. The slum exists today only because of the failure of the city to protect itself against gross evils and known perils. . . .

In respect to the street cleanliness and adequate air-space, Chicago may well take a lesson from Berlin, where the streets are kept clean by daily washings. . . .
                    —Daniel Burnham, *Plan of Chicago,* 1909

The Mexicans were the second chunk of the crowd. They seeped into Pilsen in the teens, leaving behind the Mexican revolution. Since then their numbers had grown but the stability of the colony was unknown. They worked and they kept out of politics. So Chicago hardly knew they existed. During the sixties, some Latins had copied the Black Panthers and gained some media attention as the Brown Berets. The boom in Mexican heroin in the seventies had harvested a few more headlines. But in the main, the city did not notice their presence and learned with surprise in the late seventies that a taco-fueled metropolis was rising on Twenty Sixth Street.

We came here on November 23, 1916; we were 17 solos in box cars. But the box cars had bedbugs and were cold, so I got an apartment. I met a Mexican family named E—— at 816 S. Clinton. They were acrobats in a circus and had lived in Chicago for many years. In 1917, I sent money to my mother and sister for tickets to come to Chicago. I bought the furniture of a Mexican married to an American who was getting a divorce, and we hired a cook and started a boarding house for Mexican laborers at 415 S. Halsted. The E——s also had boarders who were mostly actors. When the laborers went to them for board, they sent them to us. . . .

Some of my young boarders went south after they made some money, got their families, and returned to Chicago. They rented places they found empty near us, and started boarding houses. Some of their boarders did the same, and that is the way the Mexican colony was built here.
                                 —from Paul S. Taylor, *Mexican Labor*
                                                      In the U.S., 1928

Presumably, these pioneers are long gone from spots like Pilsen. All neighborhoods share one characteristic: people will do anything to get out of them. A long list of things will set them in motion. They feel pushed out by people with other religions, languages, colors, jobs, incomes. They feel the pull of the earth beckoning them to a house, a bit of lawn. The boys join the army and never come home. A break in finding a decent job, a good-looking woman on the far side of town, almost anything can overcome the power of the neighborhood.

After the Great Fire of 1871 the change in the character of the neighborhood and the corresponding change in the inhabitants went on rapidly; the Americans largely gave place to the Irish and the Germans, who in turn receded before the advancing hosts of Russian Jews and Italians, who still later gave way before the Greeks and Bulgarians, who are now in turn being superceded by Mexicans and Negroes. . . .

—Edith Abbott, *The Tenements of Chicago,* 1931

The Mexicans did most of the talking at the meeting. One young guy wanted to know how come when they were building Benito Juarez, the high school you know, well, when it was going up, and he walked over there, you know, thinking about how maybe like there'd be some work for him there, it being a high school in a Mexican neighborhood for Mexican kids it kind of figured, and so he asked for a job and nobody gave him one, nobody gave him nothing. Well, what about that?

A couple of young women who had worked for the alderman in the past asked him what had he done for the neighborhood, for the community, for the barrio, and did he respect the local organizations and the local people? He had better because they were getting organized and he had to pay attention to them or else.

The parish priest chomped on his cigar and periodically tried to get the meeting back on the rails and aimed at the brewery. But it seemed to have a cranky life of its own and kept reverting to complaints, demands and yells. The alderman loved it; he ate meetings like this for breakfast.

The third group in the basement did not say much. They were the cause of the meeting, but the meeting was not their cause. They were white, college educated, and many made good money. They were not born in Pilsen, did not have to live in Pilsen and would not die in Pilsen. Some welded scraps of metal together and called it sculpture. Others pummelled clay into pots; a bunch splashed colors on squares of canvas. A few sat at slant tables under fluorescent lights drawing lines so that masons, carpenters, electricians and plumbers would know where to go.

They liked Pilsen, they said. It wasn't the schools, few had children. Cheap rents and houses drew them to the district. Their arrival immediately doubled or tripled rents, but still the prices seemed cheap to them. A single room with a crapper and a galley kitchen got a coat of white paint, and presto, became an artist's studio. The new residents were into farming potted plants and wearing overalls. They saw the district getting better and better as more people like themselves moved in. They liked living in the city because they had tried the suburbs and the city was full of things hard to nail down, like strange food, crazy characters, street life. So they were drawn to Pilsen and with their occupation began the process of driving out the things they claimed had drawn them.

The artists had first been attracted to the area by a local developer. "This is a dying neighborhood," he explained, "but it has lots of potential, a lot of charm. Factories won't save it, though. We need a more middle-class idea, something for people to look up to . . . . My project is not just for artists but for those who like an arty tone." Once in awhile, the local Mexicans and local Bohemians would grasp what a more middle-class idea meant for them—higher rents and evictions—and they would be hostile to the artists for a while. This left the artists puzzled.

But normally this did not occur. Just as the artists seemed blind to the fact that their macrame world destroyed the funk that teased and tickled their walk on the wild side, the locals had a hard time finding anything wrong with fixing up old buildings. Suddenly, out of the Chicago gray had come this scheme to take an old brewery and make it a mixed media

center—a phrase as meaningful as the tooth fairy to most of the
people in the audience. Advocates of jazzing up the brewery
thought in sentences like this: "Originally, the powerhouse had
a tall, metal, heavily guyed smokestack of large diameter near
the tower; it has since been removed, improving the appearance
of the building."

A local factory owner saw the old complex differently. "It's a
real dump," he pointed out, "a haven for the worst the city has
to offer: rats as big as cats, gangs, garbage dumped in the
basement, illegal businesses, you name it." Having been used in
turn as a glue factory and pickle factory, the floors were coated
with chemicals and salts. Corrosive fluids ate out the pipes. He
did not see how a mixed media center would improve an industrial district, just as the Mexicans and Bohemians increasingly sensed that all this fixing-up would end up giving
them the boot. The crowd couldn't really argue it out, but they
felt that urban renewal, capital improvements, all that kind of
stuff, did not improve their lives. They sensed that the city
trailing behind the bulldozers and downtown plans was not a
better city, but rather someone else's city.

> The buildings of the Peter Schoehofen Brewing Company
> form an historical district. One is particularly struck by the
> cohesiveness of the buildings in their design and function
> when one steps back and views this entity from a distance.
> . . . They appear as a monument to the early brewing in-
> dustry, an empire formed by a single man's energies and
> visions, and a symbol of the rewards of the American belief
> in hard work.
> —Nomination Form, National Register of
> Historic Places Inventory, 1978

For some in the crowd the brewery was another kind of
symbol. They were the people called organizers. They were

Mexican and Bohemian and God knows what, and they plotted to control events in Pilsen. They ran the work gangs under the Comprehensive Employment and Training Act (CETA); they stimulated neighborhood associations; they went to meetings.

They smoked too much, fed daily on government rules, regulations and guidelines, and spoke in circles while searching for straight lines. Their offices were often dumps and their daily tasks could never be explained to the outside world except under the blanket term of organizer. They invented organizations that were always a random row of initials, and these alphabet outfits passed the time conferring with others of similar bent. They lived a separate culture from those they professed to organize; generally lacking families, they led families, generally lacking work, they led workers. But no one ever called them on this. The city was such a goddam mess that, cop or robber, everyone understood that things needed to be organized. So the organizers were accepted, grudgingly, as part of the city landscape.

They came to this meeting with scenarios gleaned from books or past experiences. A kind of home movie ran in their heads in which the crowd grasps the essential issue, seizes upon the contradictions banging around the neighborhood, raises their consciousness and generally gets pissed off, and then (here the music gets louder) takes over. Or, in an alternative ending at least takes a step down that endless road to power, self rule and a better life. The plot devices vary with the organizer. Some feel everything starts with a rent strike or a boycott of a local merchant. Some can imagine nothing smaller than storming the Winter Palace. For some it is Rosa Parks, for others 1917.

For all it is eventually bitter. This city has been grinding up organizers for over a hundred years. Smashed their skulls during the railway strike of 1877 leaving their gray brains on the pavement. Hung them high for the Haymarket bombing. Stomped their asses for striking against Mr. George Pullman. Busted their chops for integration marches, antiwar bullshit. Taught everyone a lesson at the 1968 Democratic Convention. Said shoot to kill when things got out of hand. Organizers in this city earned combat ribbons.

Through it all, the organizers kept their ideas alive. Take the meeting in Pilsen. They felt that the rehabilitation of old dumps by affluent whites was bad for the neighborhood because it made poor people move. Why not fix up things for poor people and then everyone can stay in place? They knew the alderman was a criminal who lived in a skyscraper in the Loop, and they knew that he did not give a damn about the people in Pilsen. What were needed were connections. Connections between old dumps being fixed up for affluent whites and not for poor people; connections between dirty streets and a dirty alderman; connections between urban renewal and urban removal; connections between 1877, 1886, 1894, 1917 and today.

All this was possible with time and patience. Just ask the right questions, in the right order, at the right place, at the right moment. Then people would begin to begin. Then the past would end and we would start anew.

Connections.

The meeting banged to order. A short, ill-tempered man wearing good clothes took over. The alderman. The crowd, what with the organizers, the priest and the time to kill, had prepared an endless list of questions. He slashed this nattering to three. He had no time for militants, outsiders, bickering, aimless bitching. What the hell, everyone knew him, and he knew them, right? Okay. Let's stop this stuff with the chicken-shit questions; nobody's trying to hide anything; no secrets here. No problem. Want to know about the brewery, right?

Okay, here's the man from the planning department, straight from downtown and he'll tell you everything you want to know. Give him a chance and you'll find there is nothing to fret about. Anytime anybody wants to do anything for the neighborhood, no problem. Okay? Want to know something? Just ask, and you'll know. We're not strangers, right? You people know me, right? Okay. Now here's the man from the planning department, now listen good, he'll tell you everything and look close at his maps, okay? Everybody's getting all riled up about nothing.

Okay?

The planner wore a suit, glasses, and a grin. He explained that all the proper steps had been taken for the project. There had been public notice and public meetings and input and output. The small plan being considered for the brewery and some of the neighboring factories and a few chunks of blighted housing fit into a big plan splashed across the walls downtown. Behind suggestions of historic preservation, mixed media centers, better housing, and more industry was something large and awe inspiring: The Master Plan To Revitalize The City of Chicago.

Now the buildings in the area under consideration were colored different hues, depending upon their fate. Consider all the squares of color together and a pattern of reason emerged. Here the planner all but took flight, racing his pointer across the map so that purples and greens and oranges and yellows and blues fused and flowed in a symphony of form and vibrancy. For a moment, a weave of city came into the room that was beyond objection. No one stirred in the wonder of it all, and no one really connected it with Pilsen, anymore than the people downtown believed a real link between the master plan and the actual city.

The main portion of the brewery would be demolished, he noted. The complex was so big and well built, no one could think what to do with it except brew beer. The power house would be saved for the time being for purposes now unknown. Space gained by destroying houses and the old factory would provide room for the other industries in the area. Now these factories had come downtown and told the planners, he said, that they had to have space or they would have to leave town.

Suburbs.

Nobody wanted that of course, we must keep jobs in Pilsen. Now, he continued, there's been a lot of questions about housing going into the site, mixed media centers, studios, historic preservation, you name it. Nothing of the sort is planned at present. Not at all. Here, and he stabbed the map with his pointer, this factory lot is going to expand this way, this one that way and so forth. What we have here is a simple proposal to accommodate the needs of local light industry, and nothing more. Okay?

The crowd was quiet for a moment as the maps loomed over them; how could they quarrel? Which way is North? The meeting slipped away from their anger and toward their confusion and the indifference of staying alive. Apparently nothing wicked was afoot. Can you see through those maps? The organizers sat making chains of cigarettes, the brewery failed to be a bludgeon to heighten consciousness or other wonders and remained an old brewery. The media center and the spectre of artists remained as they had been, no larger than a man's fist.

The meeting slipped away, the crowd hungry for a moment that never came. Hungry for the breakout, for that sharp instant when someone stands up and says it is all my doing, I'm responsible for everything rotten and stinking in your life. No garbage pickup? Your high school a rat hole? Sewers backed

up? Stores charge too much? Roof leak? Furnace broken? I did
it. Somebody paint FUCK YOU on your garage door? Park unsafe? Me again. The crowd had wanted that kind of moment
when someone would bundle up all their anxieties and disap-
pointments and angers and make them his burden. The clear
moment of anger when someone climbs into the cartoon that
plays constantly in their heads and acts out their fantasy of
revenge. But it had not happened this night.

The artists had remained meek and quiet. The alderman was
an expert in handling neighborhood complaints, and the voices
had never penetrated his arrogance. The city planner dined on
neighborhood groups daily. The people in the shadows pushing
for historic preservation of the brewery and its rebirth as a
mixed media center remained in the shadows.

People milled around awhile and then fell away into the
evening. The neighborhood's flats and apartments swallowed
them up as they drifted off under the lonely trees. A few stores
were open, the corner bar glowed with a couple of whores
waiting by the curb, but it was cold out and the street life was
gone for the season. Nobody sat on the stoops, no kids hollered
in the alleys. In just a few moments dark Chicago devoured the
light of the meeting.

There are so many ways to explain away such meetings. Cities
are said to hold a million stories, tales for filling newspaper
columns, things to say over beers after work. People keep bins
full of these anecdotes, obscenities, racial hatreds. When
something comes up, they just reach in, grab whatever is handiest and use it. Then they can handle things. Just hook a handle
to an event. Just tag a race to a face.

Handle it, handle it.

A paymaster expressed an opinion which though unusual

in some details was fairly representative in its general judgement:

The Mexicans do the work and say very little. If they are not satisfied, they come and get their pay and say nothing.

The Italians are always suspicious and think we are trying to cheat them out of time and/or money.

The Greeks come into this office drunk lots of times; the Mexicans never that I can remember. The Mexicans are as good or better than the Italians. They are much more reliable than the Greeks. The Greeks are always fighting, drunk, and kniving each other.

When it comes to building up a new track the Irish could do it better than the others. The old German and Irish crews could certainly lay out the ties and spike on the rails better than any I have seen. But they are all gone; they are policemen or firemen.

—Paul S. Taylor, *Mexican Labor*
In the U.S., 1928

When you are young, the men sit in the back yard soaking up the sun and the beer; or maybe on the front stoop. Gray days drive them to the kitchen table. They drink from quart bottles and argue with shrugs about the changes taking place where they live and where they work. They teach you about micks, guineas, kikes, niggers, spics, bohunks, polacks, you name it. They say Chicago is the place where things get made, not some goddam New York full of fag magazines and people that sell and never make anything at all. Chicago pounds, hammers, hacks, cuts, slaughters, forges, bangs, machines, wires, welds, gouges, stacks, shoves, ships. Makes. And if you can't make it here, you can't make it. Period.

The air is dirty. So is the river. So what. The government is full of thieves that don't know what work is; cops take bribes, you'd better believe it; the blacks want more and more, more houses, more ground, more jobs. Everything stinks.⌉

This is Chicago, the city that works, so go to work. Meetings? Don't go. Urban renewal, housing projects, maps with colors and squares and everything clean and clear? Are you kidding? You don't live in those maps, you escape from them. You know they will never fix this place up, they will never make the river run clean, the air smell sweet, and you know who they are. Them.

The Loop? The Art Institute? That other museum along the lakeshore? Forget it. The yacht harbor? Don't swallow that crap about the lake front and how pretty it is and better than anywhere else on earth. Turn away from those postcards showing the skyline stabbing up from the waters. How you going to see it? Stand on a wave? Look, you live here and you work there and the rest just isn't. Going to spend a week or two soaking up culture at the Institute? Working on the perfect tan by the Lake? The beaches? The beaches are bullshit. You think a man goes to work and rides the CTA and then zips home, grabs his towel, trunks and snorkel and hightails it for the beach? Look, you're a kid, you got the time, how many days you spend at the beach last summer?

The glass apartments blocking the lake air from the rest of the city and stuffed with faggots and assholes and security systems, you think you're going to raise a family in one of those? They're not for kids or families or anything really. They're addresses, not places to live.

All that stuff is wrapping, glitter for the publicity shots and politicians' wind. False front. But the city, this city is about guts. You get a job, you find a place to live where the old lady won't get raped on the way to the super, where your kids can go to school without shouldering a musket, okay? Forget the mayor, the machine, the cops, the urban renewal, the community development, the bullshit in the slick magazines. This city is straight streets that all look the same, stores, and maybe, maybe you can get near a safe park. You go to work. You come home. There's the weekends. And you save. You don't try to fix it or save it. It is fixed, it is saved. It's a big mill where people work and whatever you may think, it was a hell of a lot worse. Christ, the sky was worse, the ground was worse, the sewers spilled shit all over hell and creation, the air stunk, the river was worse, the houses were worse, the jobs were worse, the cops were worse, even the goddamn government was worse. So don't get all hot and bothered about fixing it. This city used to be as crooked as a barrel of guts.

The blacks? They're animals, and if they are not, so what? You going to give them your job, your house? Work. Save. Duck. Stay away from the plans and solutions. Let the liberals integrate or whatever; they don't have your paycheck. Don't listen to the talk and the blueprints about how nice Chicago's going to be. They lie. You take care of your own.

And don't complain.

Chicagoans, for instance, commonly believed that many men killed in the South Works were secretly buried. It was, the Chicago *Tribune* cried, 'a Centre of Mill Horrors.' Possibly as a result of these rumors, William Hard investigated the South Chicago plant and published his findings in the November 1907 issue of *Everybody's Magazine.* Its title established the central point of the article: 'Making Steel and Killing Men.' There had been in 1906 46 fatalities, and probably 2000 injuries.

—David Brody, *Steelworkers in America: The Non Union Era,* 1960

This is the way to get a handle on things, this is the way to street wisdom. To be wise is to know what you don't know, can't know, won't know. Like a chant of curses, it smothers your anger as the El screams around a curve, iron on iron, pulls you through the stall of traffic as the Dan Ryan Expressway becomes a parking lot. Turn inward or what's out there will eat you alive. Stay in the neighborhood.

Neighborhood? An idea bigger than definition and without any sure borders. Small enough to defend, big enough to live in. That's the hope. The meeting in Pilsen over the ancient brewery's fate was like all such meetings, a veritable hymn to neighborhood. As the alderman and the planner laid out their plans and peddled their contempt for everything and everyone in the neighborhood, they filled the air with a din of sacred references to the good of the neighborhood, the harmony of the neighborhood, the old neighborhood, the new neighborhood, THE NEIGHBORHOOD. The people responded. They said they lived within certain lines, and they wanted peace and security and quiet. Pilsen, they called it Pilsen, seizing the name left by early Bohemians and branded into the map by sociologists. What will this do for the neighborhood?

What will this do to the neighborhood?

He took a meditative puff on his stogey, and informed himself that time was a funny thing. Old Man Time just walked along and he didn't even blow a How-do-you-do through his whiskers. He just walked on past you. Things just change. Chicago was nothing like it used to be, when over around St. Ignatius Church and back of the yards were white men's neighborhoods, and Prairie Avenue was a toney street where all the swells lived like Fields . . . and the niggers and whores had not roosted around Twenty Second Street and Fifty Eighth Street was nothing but a wilderness . . . and there were no automobiles and living was dirt cheap . . .

Anyway there was going to be no hitches in the future of his kids. And the family would have to be moving soon. When he'd bought this building, Wabash Avenue had been a nice, decent, respectable street for a self-respecting man to live with his family. But now, well, the niggers and kikes were getting in, and they were dirty. . . . He'd sell and get out . . . and when he did he was going to get a pretty penny on the sale. . . .

—James Farrell, *Studs Lonigan*

City geography of river, street, mill, railroad, and expressway, with neighborhood what's left in between the commercial schemes. Forget the charts of the sociologists or the ZIP code bureaucrats or the politicians, and find neighborhood in a private geography of flat, store, saloon, job, maybe church, sometimes park, usually school. A place understood with one's own eyes, hands and feet, ground measured and experienced at the level of daily life. Finally, the most tangible place in the entire city because here, and only here, the messages and warnings flashed across the television, blared from the radio, splashed on the front page can register or not register, be felt or not felt. Exist or not exist.

Humans stand in a smoky church basement and speak of Pilsen and plead for Pilsen and the dream for Pilsen. Chicago, dubbed the city of neighborhoods because the small, amorphous units work as a currency that most humans in the city can physically perceive, real coin as opposed to the paper money of ward lines, and urban renewal plans, and predatory Chicago plans. Finally, neighborhood became a way to talk the city and not describe it, to argue the city and not know it, to deal with the city and not deal with it at all. But rather to deal with a myth of private, secure, nourishing turf called neighborhood. Neighborhood acts as a drug and befuddles the mind and paragraphs flow into the slick magazines by the bale. Here, look at one.

> Perhaps more than any other urban area, Chicago is a city of neighborhoods. A visitor could walk blindfolded the length of Halsted Street at the dinner hour on a summer evening and easily guess the ethnic aromas and accents of its residents . . . Polish, Black, Irish, Greek, Mexican, German, Chinese. Above all, diversity is Chicago's major charm.
>
> —Dale Wittner, Chicago, *Adventure Road,*
> Amoco Motor Club, Summer, 1979.

Jane Addams saw this same Halsted Street.

> Halsted Street is thirty two miles long, and one of the great thoroughfares of Chicago; Polk Street crosses it midway between the Stockyards to the South and the ship building yards on the north branch of the Chicago River. For the six miles between these two industries the street is lined with shops of butchers and grocers, with dingy and gorgeous saloons, and pretentious establishments for the sale of ready made clothing. Polk Street, running west from Halsted grows rapidly more prosperous; running a mile east to State Street, it grows steadily worse and crosses a network of vice on the corners of Clark Street and Fifth Avenue. Hull House once stood in the suburbs . . . and its site now has corners on three or four foreign colonies. . . .
>
> The idea underlying our self-government breaks down in such a ward. . . .
>
> —Jane Addams, *Twenty Years at*
> *Hull House,* 1910.

The idea underlying self-government breaks down in such a ward because the neighborhoods lack a permanent population committed to a permanent place. Neighborhoods lack neighbors. The place of shifting borders has a shifting content. As one of the real estate speculators in Pilsen put it, "Families leave this area as soon as they get some extra money. The only rental market left here is young men, groups of three to six, who are trying to get enough money so they can get new cars and leave." This is the rule, not the exception. In the corner of the kitchens that charmed the travel magazine writer is a packed suitcase. And this transiency is not a characteristic of just poor neighborhoods. This is what neighborhoods are, have been, and promise to be. The idea is not easily accepted.

> A confrontation between members of the Latin Disciples and Latin Kings street gangs left two young men badly beaten early Monday. . . . One neighborhood resident said the two men's screams could be heard blocks away. . . . "The park is in Disciple's territory," one policeman said. "The Kings are looking for trouble if they go into that neighborhood."
>
> —*West Side Times-Lawndale News,*
> July 26, 1979

Neighborhood gets confused with the European village. The European village was a place where your ancestors were buried and where you would be buried and your children would be buried. You lived in their house, you sat in their chairs. You died in the same bed that you were conceived in. That was the image. Whatever its truth in Europe, it had precious little in the New World. Here people did not stay put. Even the industrial city of North America differed from that of Europe.

The London of 1880 that headed the world's largest empire had a population where 64 out of every hundred were born in the city, where 94 out of 100 were either native or from England and Wales, 98 out of 100 included as place of birth Great Britain or Ireland. Only 1.6% of the great city's people came from beyond the British Isles. That same year in the United States, foreign born and the children of foreign born per hundred ran 78 in San Francisco and St. Louis, 80 per hundred in Cleveland and New York, 84 in Detroit and Milwaukee and 87 in Chicago. This at a time when migration had hardly begun.

The folk movements of the nineteenth century were global movements but they became particularly intense in the cities of America. And within this urban movement operated a neighborhood movement. This motion has never really ceased. The idea of the village asserts that experience and geography have the same borders. Neighborhoods were and are temporary places full of temporary people. They are designations and handles for the schemes of politicians, planners and political scientists—things like freeways, housing projects, schools, factories—but they are not a commitment of families to a place through time; nor have they ever been.

There have been demographic stalls and spurts that can mislead. During the Depression and the Second World War, many people were locked in place only to stampede to the suburbs when peace came. But the hundred year pattern is clear, and that pattern is constant movement into and out of the neighborhoods as people attempt to better their lives. When people today come face to face with urban renewal or school busing or freeways or whatever and speak of neighborhood as something fundamental and stable, they do it in ignorance of the past and in violation of the reality of the present.

American's urban population has always been highly mobile. In fact, there has been an almost 85 percent neighborhood turnover in cities in the early twentieth century. . .

Of course it is true that there are neighborhoods where some residents have lived their entire lives. But this kind of neighborhood rootedness has been more the exception than the rule. Most real estate brokers, even in the most stable neighborhoods, report that each home changes ownership about every seven years. In a 1972 survey of over 1600 residents in seven New York City neighborhoods, 55 percent of the residents said they wanted to move out of the area they lived in; within two years 45 percent had moved. . . .
>   —John M. Goering and Edward T. Rogowsky,
>   "The Myth of the Neighborhods,"
>   *New York Affairs,* 1978.

But the word remains an indestructible piety, shared at a meeting like the one in Pilsen by alderman and audience and organizers. The greater the human movement the shriller the insistence on the ideal of the neighborhood. In Chicago, the thinking and the dollars went into the transportation of goods, the buying and the selling, the sweat of noisy factories, the power of iron horses, boats, trucks. Neighborhoods slipped in between the smokestacks and rails and canals. They were and are brief accidents that occurred outside the planner's order and the entrepreneurial goals of the city. From time to time they are discovered like strange bugs under a rock.

The Great Fire of 1871 drove reporters into the belly of the city in their coverage of the blaze. For many, this journey was almost an exploration of discovery into a savage unknown land. "The fire," one wrote, "had already advanced . . . through the frame buildings that covered the ground thickly north of Dekoven Street and east of Jefferson Street—if those miserable alleys shall be dignified by being denominated streets. That neighborhood had always been a *terra incognita* to respectable Chicagoans, and during a residence of three years in the city I had never visited it." This thrill of discovery has become a Chicago tradition popping up with every world's fair or major hoopla. In 1968, the roadway from the downtown hotels to the Amphitheater had to be spruced up with wooden fences lest delegates to the Democratic convention see some of the neighborhoods.

Politically, no one can leave the beloved neighborhoods, even if visitors must be shielded from the sight of them. The late Mayor Daley made a bit of national fame out of remaining in the Bridgeport of his birth. Aldermen also keep within the borders of their fiefdoms.

> Mayor Jane Byrne paid a call on Ald. Edward R. Vrdolyak (10th) last night, surprising many of some 800 guests who feasted on barbequed lamb and pig under a circus tent in the alderman's back yard. . . .
>
> Vrdolyak took Byrne and her husband through the imposing multilevel home that dwarfs surrounding bungalows in the modest working class neighborhood. Inside, a carpeted spiral staircase connects three levels of the expansive living room. There is a fireplace at either end of the room and a white piano in the center.
>
> Vrdolyak showed the tennis courts built recently on the alley he acquired behind his home. He showed her his gazebo, and then she sat down at one of the 400 seats he had set under a giant green and blue striped circus tent in another part of the yard.
>
> Nearby visitors were lining up to be served steak, and meat from the three lambs and a pig that were roasted on the grounds. Others gathered around the two bars in the yard.
> —*Chicago Sun Times,*
> July 11, 1979

The talk at the Pilsen meeting is thwarted by words everyone shares and everyone believes and no one quite understands. The people at the top and the people at the bottom were equally dependent on certain figurative language. Aldermen may retire to their castles, the local citizenry may toil daily to get the wherewithal for flight from the district, and the organizers may spend hours arguing about what a sham the city of neighborhoods is, but without the myth and the vocabulary, they all go mute. God, they babble, Chicago has to be about neighborhoods. It's not New York, even the aldermen live in the neighborhoods, look even Daley stayed in Bridgeport. Hell, people live in the neighborhoods.

Waving the word everyone arrives at the neighborhood, some to take their cut because they have political power, some to dream condominiums or mixed media centers, some to push for urban renewal so that strange maps can be fulfilled, some to organize humans into units that seize power. They all come to the neighborhood to rule it or rob it or raise revolution or taxes or high rises or funk or prevailing level of the arts in these parts. The myth of the neighborhood as a coherent, powerful and nourishing place becomes the prison that stops the top and the middle and the bottom from looking honestly at the city and realizing this is not a haven for residential districts. The past still rules in Chicago and the dead still reckon. The meeting and the meetings and the crowd and the crowds strive to restore districts to conditions that never prevailed in the past, struggle to maintain a level of stability unknown by previous generations, and seek sustenance in the streets that legions before them could not find.

Heads abuzz with confusion and a six-pack under arm, it was off to a nearby apartment to discuss and destroy whatever sense had passed between the alderman, the city planner, and the people of Pilsen. It was over the beers that the talk of the shotgun and other matters crept out into the light of the artist's living quarters and workshop.

The man lived in a store that no longer sold anything. A two-story shoebox wedged into a row of shoeboxes on Halsted, the place was tarpapered and plain outside. The shop windows on the ground floor were frosted glass. Next door, a similar house listed badly toward the north pole. Like most buildings in Chicago, the structure looked innocent of an architect. Most of the homes and businesses in Chicago were thrown up by the time and motion school: how much bang for how many bucks how fast? This school dominated almost everything outside the Loop and the ancient wooden building on Halsted was representative of its achievements.

Open the front door and a carpeted stairway climbs to the second floor; in times past the family lived here, busy pinching pennies over the business. The dream dictated saving enough money and sweating the wife and kids so that one could eventually move to a separate residence. Now, in the late seventies, the building was returning to the strategy of its originators. The man was an artist, the first floor his studio, upstairs his home. The space of the business remained one room, gently penetrated by an oak rail from its heyday years ago as an insurance office or real estate base. Touch the oak and you magically saw the place busy with men in detachable collars, and young girls bent over machines punching out letters, all moving to the beat of the rotarian commerce that once thumped in the place. Now easels, paint pots, brushes, sketches, neutral light filled the scene. Very neat, a workman's place for sure.

Up the stairs and more of the same feeling. He was good with his hands, and so the floors, the walls, the wood trim, the doors, every surface looked perfectly restored. More than restored. The builders in the 1880s took less care, had less time and money. Old light fixtures were replaced by chrome spots that drove back the shadows and lit up the paintings. A huge canvas dominated the main room with a violent pink. A monstrous dog loomed, mouth open, crocodile teeth shiny. JUNK YARD DOG. Then the name, and the date.

Everyone sprawled around a low refinished table and for awhile the only sound was the popping of beer tabs. The meeting had been a bust for many, for nothing had gone according to plan. No confrontation meant no release, and the residue was a sensation of frustration. The game was over but there had never been a ninth inning. So everyone sits and drinks. The painter who had made the walls and floors come to life for the first time in decades, was very nervous. It was ten o'clock and his teenage daughter was not home yet. He did not trust Pilsen nights. There was a problem with Pilsen days, for that matter.

You don't advertise a fixed-up place like this. Make the storefront windows opaque; the natives are restless. They might see things you have that they do not have. That was part of the reason that buildings with new innards kept their old hides. But there was another motive for making urban renewal on an individual basis a closet drama.

> Walsh soon sold the building. If he hadn't, he would have gone broke trying to meet the city building department's demands for improvements. Chicago has one of the nation's strictest building codes. Although rarely enforced, it provides City Hall with a powerful club over property owners.
>
> —Mike Royko, *Boss*

Work done on the exterior of a building drew flies, just like the other stuff. The painter said you don't do anything on the outside because they'll notice. Tom, an architect, a man pouring his treasure and spare time into fixing a place in Pilsen, seconded this notion. The thing had layers, lots of layers. They could break you if you went with the code, and they could break you if you went without the code. It all depended on your attitude.

Everybody knew what could happen if you pasted the wrong political poster in your window in a well-organized ward. The boys would come from downtown, and Goddamn, your $80,000 two-flat with airconditioning, wall-to-wall carpeting, two-car garage, finished basement, central heating, oak floors, working fireplaces, two baths, and leather tooled wet bar—why, the place is a hovel, a threat to life and limb. Look buster, this place has got to get a new exit. There, punch it right through that second floor brick wall. And it's gonna need a fire escape too—don't want anybody fried in a fire, do we? Now, let's check the wiring. . . .

The city's lust for structural perfection could have remarkable spin-offs. The bar on the corner, the one just down the block from the painter's house, well, they went nuts, temporarily insane, and put the wrong candidates' mug in the window during a recent demonstration of democracy. At high noon, just like in the movies, a car stopped in front of the bar, double-parked you know, and this guy got out with, oh, about a 34-ounce Louisville slugger in his right hand. He set himself up real good in the warm sun, and before you knew it he'd hit a bunch of home runs. Presto, you had one of them open air saloons, the kind the stewardesses love in the swinging new town called Old Town. Then he got back in the car and carefully drove off with his wonder stick.

These were some of the preliminary layers of frustration facing any local home owner or home restorer. Don't let them know what you are doing, and don't make them mad. But if you peeled deeper into the thing, nothing got easier. Essentially, the city building department and the police levied a tax on human effort to change the walls, floors, ceilings, wires, pipes, roofs, windows, doors, and cellars in Chicago. With luck you got to pay the tax into outstretched hands and went about your business molested no more. But things got tough when you tried to meet code, when, because you had angered the gods or were out of your head, you had to meet every stinking little regulation. That's when you had to grunt.

Tom and his wife paid $7000 for their small brick home. First they played clean-up. The sewage had backed up in the cellar, and Tom hand-carried 500 gallons of shit out. A little brick work here and there and soon they'd laid 13,000 bricks. All sounds like a bit of a lark for an architect, a person trained to read and follow building codes. Nope. Tom's training was his Achilles' heel; he tried to meet code.

He said the wiring alone had run him $3000.

He said, you know, well, I know these guys from work, I deal with them all the time, and Christ, I can draw up the plans, who the hell else can draw up their own plans? Cost a fortune to hire an asshole like me, so I go downtown to the department with my plans rolled up and I go here and I go there, and finally the guy knows me, and says okay and never looks at the plans. Chicago. I've lived here for years, but I met the code, in the wires, in the pipes, the whole damn thing, and it cost a fortune and I did most of the work and I drew up my own plans.

Now you take these places that that Bohunk, that local developer, is fixing up for artists. Christ, he's got a block of studios and fifty or sixty houses. You think he meets code? Shit, those places are dumps. I remember when he was fixing up the storefronts for the studios, he'd start working, ripping and attacking and hammering, and a prowl car comes by, and they say, shit, here's a guy rearranging a building and there's no permit tacked up, you know, like you're supposed to. And they pull over. God, this is wonderful. I was there. They pull over, just a couple of beat cops, and they go up to him and ask where's the permit? you know, and he starts waving his arms and jabbering and bellerin', and he says I talked to the sergeant, it's okay, I told him, and they're getting madder and madder because they don't know any of this shit about talking to the sergeant. He's out there wearing goddamn rags with grease and crap smeared all over them, and saying ask the sergeant, ask the sergeant, and telling them how he's the big landlord of Pilsen. And they look at him and he's trying to fuck them over, and goddamn, they get pissed off, but they leave. And all the time he keeps ripping and hammering, trying to close up the outside of the building before more shit hits the fan.

After a while, the sergeant comes by, and he don't know what the fuck's going on either, all he sees is this dirty Bohunk re-modeling a building with a mess of apartments on Halsted Street and he ain't go no permit, not a fucking thing. He starts the arm waving and the jabbering again, still pounding away, only now he's saying ask the captain, it's okay, just ask the captain, and the guy can't figure this out, the captain ain't told him shit, he just sees walls moving on Halsted Street and no permit. I don't know how in the hell he does it, but goddamn, after a day of arm waving and jabbering and bullshit and pounding, he's got the outside done, sealed up and he's gone private again, and he never did get a fucking permit. He's crazy. I've seen him come trotting out of an alley in a good sportcoat and nice slacks and a clean shirt clutching some goddamn piece of plumbing, a free elbow joint or something and ooze and crud dripping all over the front of him and he don't give a shit, he don't even notice. He's found something for free. He just does things. Like the way he got the alley back of his apartments. One day he just closed it off, you know a little bit, with sawhorses. Then a little bit more, then suddenly, what alley? It's gone and there's nothing there but a wall.

Sears puts up a tower for a couple of hundred million in the Loop and they get nickeled and dimed by aldermen for shutting off an alley, like nobody'd have a place to walk the dog anymore. But this Bohunk, hell, he just does it. A week or two ago, he closed off another one. Now he's just got the sawhorses up, but you wait and see, boom, he'll have it walled off. Shit, he takes alleys like the city fills in the Lake, like it's some kind of frontier just there for the taking.

But just you or I try it.

But he's got friends, born here you know, and God, you're downtown at one of those building department meetings and, hell, I was at one a month or two ago, and he walked in, and the guy chairing it, he stops everything and say well look who's here and recognizes him from the chair like he was a visiting big shot. He's got friends.

Tom knows all about the permits.

Chicago born, he delights in the city's venality as he curses it. He goes by the book and knows a lot of people don't. The city of straight streets is full of cut corners. You talk to a woman who makes spare change painting closets in highrise apartment buildings being carved into condominiums. She puts in ski boots, tennis rackets, warm-up suits, the usual gear of highrise men, so that buyers plopping down fifty or sixty grand for a two-bedroom won't notice that their haven in the sky has one closet. Then one day the developer asked her to start painting doors on the walls. Seemed odd but okay. Then she looked around. The place only had one exit.

So Tom knows all about permits and bitches and moans and laughs over his tangled investment in Pilsen. He had come here and bought because the property was dirt cheap, just like the one restored by the painter and now filling with beer cans, and the war with the city's building code was just one more tax on his investment, one more hurdle to cross in his flight from inflation and an economy that scared the hell out of anyone who looked at it too long or too close. He's been run to ground so to speak like the rest of the nation, driven to an almost religious belief that real estate would pull him through.

The mixed media center and the historic preservation and the artists, all these things were natural signs of a shift in the city. Young, single, or married and without children, middle class whites coming back in for bargains. They wanted the houses poor people lived in because they could afford them.

Anybody with brains could take a look at the vacant land, the banker's dreams of mortgages, mortgages, mortgages and the migratory drift of single whites scenting the wind for bargain housing and big city funk and know Pilsen and all the other Pilsens were squatting in front of a steamroller. Look at the big state university a mile away. Look at the business towers penetrating the monoxide muck of the Loop. Hell, anybody knew and everybody knew that Pilsen was putting tortillas behind it and going more for crepes.

Tom knew.

He wasn't seizing his ground by the river for his golden years. Why should he? No one ever had. The Bohemians had marched toward Cicero and, regardless of what he did, the Mexicans would be off for other parts eventually. No, Tom bought into Pilsen as a sort of station of the Cross on the path to financial absolution. The house with the basement cleaned out of shit and the sanded oak floors and the new wiring and plumbing might be urban renewal to urbanologists or the invasion of the middle class to local organizers, but in Tom's private movie it was just a step toward putting his life together, an investment. He tosses down the beers and talks of Pilsen and talks of his travels for his architectural firm in the Loop that pays his bills. Christ, a few weeks ago he had to go down to Tennessee or some such place to read the blueprints to a construction crew for a week or two.

Then there was New Mexico. Christ, you can't believe the stars, and the dirt and the rocks are all different colors. No people, nobody there at all. Up at the Four Corners they've got a power plant so goddamn filthy, the sky just goes black with ash, they couldn't operate it in Chicago even, this big dirty mother of a plant flinging shit into the sky out in the middle of nowhere. God, it's hard to get enough of New Mexico; growing, beautiful, empty. Tom went on and on and suddenly the stars were blazing down and light wind off the mesa was working gently on the neck and in every direction lay the look of postcards.

Tom was a new settler in Pilsen, a pioneer.
Tom had bought some land in New Mexico.

> But in the neighborhood, you were safe. . . . So for a variety of reasons, ranging from convenience to fear to economics, people stayed in their own neighborhood, loving it, enjoying the closeness, the friendliness, the familiarity, and trying to save enough money to move out.
> —Mike Royko, *Boss*

Tom recalled the night he and his wife had come home to Pilsen, they'd been off somewhere in their car, and they'd just pulled to the curb. This was before they had their house, this was when they lived in an apartment. Anyway, they'd just pulled in, and they heard something.

People wearing little brown berets were carrying rocks and clubs. They carefully smashed the windows on the front of the apartment building. Glass shards gleamed in the entryway, and clubs kept swinging and swinging. The windows kept breaking as young Mexican kids wearing brown berets swung the clubs.

Tom recalled that he started to get out, you know—what the hell's going on here? sort of thing—but he stopped. They were trashing the place he and his wife lived, but he stayed put. He sensed that there was a line running down that street and he was on one side and they were on another and crossing that line would cost both of them. Nobody called the cops, nobody said anything, nobody shouted from the windows, Hey, you kids down there, hey, stop that. No sound. Just glass breaking, and crunching underfoot. They just sat there, they knew. They waited like you do at the gas station when they're filling your tank. Idly. When the job was done, and the brown hats walked off into the night, Tom and his wife got out of the car and calmly walked into their apartment building, shiny daggers reflecting light under their feet. That evening became part of the way they lived, of the rumors, the rumors and in the neighborhood of the city of neighborhoods there are always rumors, rumors of war.

Chicago's a three-sided town, north, south, and west. There's this skin of fancy apartments along the Lake with parks, expensive restaurants, Gold Coast and jogging trails. This is not Chicago. Chicago is a three sided town and on all sides you are raised for the war.

Years gone by, they used to train up a South Sider on hate and anger. They'd tell you things but never explain. Everybody understood. Come spring and the ground would go to mush and scent would rise up for the first time in months. Guys would leave the bars and put on their uniforms to smash softballs in the park. On 79th Street the heat would bake off the summer sidewalks into the women's faces as they trudged along with their cloth shopping bags. The streetcars still ruled the street. The big war was over and the Korean business just closed out and everybody was waiting for the next move. Things were good, so good for the first time in a long time. Ashland Avenue clogged on the summer evenings with convertibles cruising with their tops down. It seemed like all you could smell was food.

You'd hear things. Some of them had moved into a place down on 74th a while back. They bought a house. First the porch was dynamited. They left before the second act.

Church names mark your land into fiefdoms: St. Sabina's, St. Rita's, St. Leo's. You get hurt, you go to Little Company of Mary's. Want to party? Wait for St. Patrick's day. Thousands of men, women and children crushed together for that one; people like Ed Sullivan would fly out to be the Grand Marshall. All the floats, high school bands, rosary leagues and clubs form up in Foster Park. Each year a bunch of men stumble along trying to look like a military outfit; their faces are flushed with early morning shots of rye. They hold a banner as wide as 79th Street: ALL IRELAND IS NOT YET FREE. Behind them a giant rosary snakes along, guys each shouldering one of the giant beads. Kids run in and out, hop on and off the floats. Everybody has had a few. Downtown they dye the river green, trap pigeons and dye them green too. All the people say it is a great day for the Irish.

There is a dance one Saturday night at Foster Park Field House. Some of them come. Why? Don't they know they're not wanted? What do they want? When they leave they find the windows on their cars have been smashed, the tires lie limp and slashed. Men are waiting with radio antennas snapped off the cars. The night is remembered as part of the local short history course. It never has a date, no names please, but it always has a flavor. We took care of them. Like 1919 when we filled the river with the bastards.

They call it the neighborhood but nobody really has a name for it. On the maps that delight the professors it seems to take in parts of Auburn Park, Englewood, Morgan Park and Ogden Park. All them parks, you'd think the place was a national forest or something. Just call it The Neighborhood. If you have to get specific, name two streets, 79th and Halsted, 80th and Loomis, like that. Some of the people have been here a long time, right through the Depression and the wars. Their Catholic schools and churches are here. They've gotten used to the park and the stores. If you get up early you can see women with scarves on their heads plodding to 6 o'clock mass, and this on weekdays.

A few people move to the suburbs after the War, and after Korea more move or get ready to move. You visit them and find that they live in houses, not apartments, and have yards all to themselves. The kids own dogs.

Back in the neighborhood, there is a new feeling in the air. The anger and hate is mixed with fear. Everyone is waiting for them to make their move. The old woman who lives in the corner apartment on the alley, the one who gives all the kids cookies, starts making noises about them. She worked for the police department for years, her brother's connected. She says she knows who is who and what is what. She begins to hold block meetings. People come and talk and have coffee and sign papers swearing that they will never sell to them, swear before God. The church, the schools, the parks, Christ, who wants to give it all to them.

They'll ruin it.

They ruin everything.

They smell.

They move into a perfectly nice place, really swell homes and look at them now, the lawns a bunch of weeds and broken bottles, garbage everywhere, old mattresses tossed down into the backyards. You drive by and you see curtains hanging out the dirty windows. And they pack in there like animals. They like it that way you know, like to live together like a bunch of pigs.

The neighbors make decisions.

A swimming pool is offered for the park by the politicians downtown.

No thanks. Might attract them.

The public school is half empty and the city wants to bus in kids from crowded neighborhoods, those neighborhoods. The principal elects to have retarded children hauled instead. Once in a while, you see one of them shopping along 79th Street. The people say they are sent. They give them money to walk around and shop, so we will see them, so we will get used to them. So we will give in.

There are always rumors, rumors of war, always of war.

The painter who restored the two-story building on Halsted Street in Pilsen, the inside not the outside, he's uncomfortable with the talk of broken glass and brown berets. People like to be pioneers after the Indians are gone. So the painter steers talk to the strange cafe a few doors down the block, the one the three brothers run, the twins and the other one.

Christ, it's a crazy place, says the painter. I mean you go in there and it's like the guys running it are nuts.

Nuts? asks Tom, Nuts? Hell, that place, that place's a bookie joint.

Well, I don't know about that, says the painter.

The hell it's not, says Tom. Christ, don't you notice the twins, I mean I go in there all the time just to hear them yell at each other, one pitching and the other catching, God, they're rough on each other, but anyway, don't you notice them on the phone, notice how they're at the phone rattling it off bang, bang, bang. Nobody else gets to use that phone, and it's a pay phone. I mean you think it's really a restaurant?

It's a crazy place, says the painter. I mean I went in there for breakfast last week and I ordered an egg, bacon, toast. And the twins were back there yelling and screaming at each other and calling each other fuckheads. God it's a crazy place, and well, they came out and served me the egg, bacon and toast on a paper towel. On a paper towel! Can you beat that? I mean this is a crazy neighborhood, these people been round here a long time some of them and they're like nuts, like inbred or something, like those people down south. I've been doing odd jobs for some extra money, carpentry and whatnot, and it gets you into some weird buildings around here. There's one old guy living in this place for years and years and so I go down into his basement to do something and his floor is buried, and I mean buried, in *shit*. His main must have broke years ago, and he just goes on, the hell with it, you know?

Fueled by beer, the talk continues, the good talk, the kind the city has always prompted, the kind that makes it bearable. Talk of where you were the night Dillinger was shot, of how the speakeasies operated, the old Kelly-Nash machine, fixing a ticket, of the time you were stopped on Lake Shore Drive in a pick-up—NO TRUCKS ALLOWED—whoops, and the cops said give us what you got in your wallet and you said okay and you only had two bucks and a few minutes later you see the goddamn red light flashing again behind you and you think, what the hell? And they pull you over and one gets out and walks up to the driver's side and throws the bucks, crumpled up, into your lap and says, Christ, if this is all you're carrying you must need it, and he walks away. Talk so nobody looks. Talk so nobody says anything.

Then there are the flames climbing walls and eating buildings. Flickering everywhere but mainly behind the red lines drawn by insurance men who stick to maps and stay off the street. For the painter, for Tom, for the organizers, for everyone, the fires are in Pilsen. They flash in the nightmares of the Bohemian landlord with his dozens of houses, and they gleam on the edge of the organizers' vision. Beneath the talk, in the silent pauses, people feel the heat of the flame. The painter lives next door to one of the landlord's houses and he is afraid that Pilsen anger will torch it and he will go up in smoke with the anger.

One Sunday morning a huge church burns, an old monster church now gone to neglect and black Baptist worship. Everyone says it was set. No need to check, to sift the ashes. Had to be set. After all this is Pilsen, what more proof do you need. A fourteen-year-old girl says it was set, had to be, everybody hates them, everyone knows that. So, a building maybe seventy or eighty years old burns on a cold Sunday morning before services start. Burns with only the deacon down in the basement firing up the ancient boiler that the strapped congregation can never even dream of replacing, and the boiler sends wisps of warm air through the old duct work and something gives out, gives up, a spark, a flame and the place is gone.

But everyone says it was set.

Had to be set.

This is Pilsen, you know.

Arson, always arson.

Rumors.

Always rumors.

Sometimes the rumor is fact. The organizers have their eye on a building. They've been sitting around pooling various federal funds and state funds in their heads and they think they can buy it and fix it up as good, reasonable housing. One night the place goes up in smoke. They think the guy next door lit it, think he wants the lot vacant for parking. The cops are not interested. They say the forms take forever, and what is the difference? Everyone argues for two hours at curbside. The cops do not give in. The gas can sits there empty on the sidewalk.

This is the noise of everyday life in the city. Events refuse to form into a meaning and when they do, when you find the gas can in the smoking ruins, nobody will pay attention to you. This is the second city. Here the laws get bent, and all the plans and programs announced downtown remain downtown, uptown or out of town. In the second city things do not get better; things get crazy. The connection between city plans and goals and city streets is very hard to make if you live on these streets. You are supposed to have fire protection, you are told to do this and that by the fire chief. And then you stand on the curb with a gas can by a torched building and you are told so what. When you accept this you have grown up. When you ignore this you are a city planner.

The second city is the one people live in. They do not understand what is going on, and they have stopped listening. They have retreated to complaint or indifference or myth.

What caused that?

THEY CAUSED THAT.

Who is they?

THEM.

Hating is easier than thinking. Weakness is less tiring than wrestling for power. So people hate and are weak. Better to forget than to remember; remembering never got anyone anywhere. That's what everyone says.

Tom knows all this, the painter knows all this, the organizer knows all this, everyone knows all this. The city is shifting under their feet into something else again, and sometimes they think, well, the city has always been change, and other times they feel that this time is different. For the first time the city is losing its ability to absorb lower class people, for the first time the only sign of growth in the city is the movement of legions of self-sterilized adults.

Yet, the place goes through the motions. Where robber barons once plotted huge factories, now wheeler dealers wage war on the poor to get some ground for condos, complete with sauna and hot tubs. Nobody dreams ports anymore, they dream marinas. If you pored over the plans and schemes being executed in this city, you would think it was the local result of an era of declining energy costs, the fruit of cheap energy and mass affluence.

Now the talk finally gets around to the shotgun. After a lot of beer and a sudsy tour of the building code, a review of the meeting, a look at the local ethnography, after brave words on the city's economy and lack of one, of syndicate alderman and old Bohunks with broken sewer mains, of New Mexico and the stars, the shotgun comes floating up as an Oh, by the way, sort of thing. The tale enters kind of inadvertently because no one knows quite what to make of it. That's common in Chicago where most anecdotes are punctuated and analyzed with shrugs.

You know? Eh?

  Okay?

  Okay.

  Shotguns are cold tubes. They come with barrels side by side, with tubes ventilated to release gas, with tubes chopped short so you can take it with you. They make a loud noise and give a sharp kick and you cannot miss. That is why people prefer bird guns for shooting other people. Cut a man in half, they say. Can't miss. The republic is stuffed with wives trained by husbands to fetch the bird gun from the closet, just point, aim at the widest part—you cannot miss.

  Tom did not know where the story should begin or end and where in the jumble of beer and conversation it fit. Maybe it did not mean anything. But there it was suddenly, popping up quietly among the painter's white walls and satiny oak.

  He had come from work one night late and gone into the kitchen for a beer. He heard a noise out in the alley. Two humans were holding a third human, stabbing him again and again. Tom yelled to his wife, Christ, call the cops, and then he grabbed the shotgun and went out. Later, much later, he learned the knifing followed a dance at which there had been a dispute over a girl. Offense was given and answered with knives.

  He surprised the trio at their work, and he pressed the bird gun against the skull of one human working with a knife and he said, if you move, I'll smoke you. Something like that; later it would be hard to repeat the phrase without smiling. Smoke you. Just a bit better than being at a loss for words. No one moved. They stood there in the Pilsen alley, bleeding and shaken and locked together into the same ending, just not knowing what the ending would be. Down the alley, a parked car blocked the way. The vehicle remained motionless, and so did the four humans.

Breathing and waiting. Minutes ticked by and tens of minutes. After three-quarters of an hour, the car turned on its lights and crept forward. Inside were two cops.

You see, Tom explained, they'd been waiting for it to end, waiting for it to be safe again. Then they'd come and look it over and tag the bodies.

What do you make of that, huh?

Cops. Pilsen, Christ.

Some neighborhood.

city gov't

This strictly explores non di...

front b...

4 Tooker Ciity

THE WORD
U CAN
GIVES WOMEN
MUCH ENCOURAGEMENT

Tyner was moving and the tiny cardboard sign indicated the scale of the move. He was moving a whole world, complete with philosophy, sixty pounds of garlic, and the odds and ends of civilization as we know it in Chicago. He'd been living in a loft on Dearborn Street, the old Printer's Row of the word trade just south of the Loop, and paying $200 a month for 2000 square feet. He made complicated pipes for people who smoked dope.

His loft was just north of Dearborn Park, where developers were rearing "Chicago's Next Great Neighborhood." About a mile away was Pilsen. Tyner was squatting on the dangerous ground where Chicago's big movers and shakers were currently moving and shaking. He had moved hopefully a year and a half earlier into a centrally located slum. Now God in his infinite mischief had made the area prime ground for a loft explosion. Investors, artists, big time architects, little time architects were seizing the district's old warehouses and renovating them into lofts for living and creating. The whole thing was patterned after New York's SoHo district, and some of the same boys were in on both. As a group, they had gotten the city to change the height limit on warehouse living from 55 to 80 feet—the extra thirty bringing a hell of a lot of warehouses into the fold. Now the stampede was on and Tyner and his kind were being trampled.

99

Tyner blamed the whole mess, the stampede, his having to move, on cigarettes and tits.

Tyner came into the picture through a picture. Ron lived across the street in a loft, the very kind of place that was putting Tyner into flight. The whole building was a series of condominiums for artists, old warehouse space that had been sandblasted so that the floors gleamed with beautiful wood and the ceilings looked magnificent with strong beams and the walls were flat white. A combination workshop-home with Ron's work, photography, scattered around. There was a shot of a black woman strutting her stuff at a White Sox night game. Another, of a crane demolishing a nearby building while an artist hunched over his easel. And then the shot of Tyner.

Hair tumbling down to his shoulders, slight sway to his thin body, he held a toker in each hand. His hatchet face smeared with a slight grin, like he'd stumbled onto the secret of the universe, some midwestern mantra. In the background could be discerned a complicated array of shelves, boxes, stacks and piles of things. Staring just from the left of him an old fruit box with a sticker: PROSPERITY. On the ground, a cart to pull behind his bicycle. He was barefoot, like all lay saints.

Ron the photographer had tales of Tyner the toker. Middle of the winter he walked around out there in the snow barefoot. He scrounged all his food from the South Water Street market so well that last year he spent $150 on food. A real character. Could see his place right out Ron's restored window. Two cultures in a sense. For Ron's place was part of a new wave of loft living, of rehabbing, of moving back into town. In fact, it was this very eruption of loft lust that had excited developers over the old brewery in Pilsen and fostered dreams of a mixed media center. Tyner, on the other hand, was more out of a Nelson Algren novel, a gourmet of the alleyways with a joint in his mouth, or, to be exact, one of his tokers rather than a needle in his arm. He was the kind of person doomed by any and all acts of restoration and rehabilitation.

His 2000 square feet stunk of his garlic. Scattered through the place were boxes filled with spools, plastic bags, old film canisters, wires, beads, buttons, coat hangers, straps, thread, string. Here and there a saw, a hammer, a drill, benches for the work. But mainly, 2000 square feet of boxes and bags filled with whatever Tyner found.

Tooker Ciity, a recycling center.

In a small cubbyhole was the kitchen, packed floor-to-ceiling with jars of herbs and rice and flour. And his 60-pound sack of garlic. The phone rings. Even the recycle wizard of Tooker Ciity needs a phone.

On the door the necessary sign. Tooker Ciity, of course.

There are racks of little plastic cans filled with herbs, all neatly packed and hand-lettered. Each container has a number code known but to Tyner.

790602 C*mwmiyle *197&2

790618 Peppyrmiint *35&2

But there are no sandblasted roof beams, no polished oak flooring, no white walls. The place looks like the dump it is, a nest for some strange rodent, not a haven for the up-and-coming artist and craftsman. Two thousand square feet, three solid rooms of Tyner. No easily copied style, no nothing for a photo layout. No fern, no macrame. This is a private place where a man does his work. A loft in its original sense, a sweatshop.

The device that spawned this disarray, or at least was supposed to explain it, was The Tooker. Tyner invented the devilish machine about a decade ago and since then has produced 20,000 of them. The various concoctions of herbs were for street demonstrations lest the law fall down upon his head. The Tooker was a pipe with one to eight tubes for one to eight smokers. The customer put dope in the pipe's bowl and toked.

The core of the device was a block of wood hollowed out for the plastic tubes and with a screened brass bowl for the weed. This was the precise point at which most paraphernalia ended, but Tyner had not sold 20,000 by quitting easily. His Tooker went on and on. Suspended from wires like a nest of snakes, were various extra features. On one wire, a small cuplike device for holding roaches, on another a beer tab for shoveling fuel into the pipe. A safety pin did double duty, the blunt end being a tamper, the pin for aeration. For a few cents more, the customer got the machine's more cosmic features.

A bell for the music of the spheres.

An emergency pencil for those big ideas that come to a toker in the middle of a toke.

A paper clip for holding a scrap of paper after the toker has written down those big ideas with the emergency pencil.

All these deluxe extras fastened to the Tooker by telephone wire. Where do you get telephone wire? It's everywhere. The 2000 square feet of loft renting for $200 per month filled with junk? Simply a warehouse for Tooker parts.

The Tooker itself was far more than a mass of wires and geegaws. It, like its creator, was a state of mind. For Tyner, The Tooker was no different than the Model T was to Henry Ford, a total expression of everything America hoped and dreamed. Standing there whipping wires around, his skinny frame decked out in rags and wire-rimmed glasses, his skin that strange translucent quality of the total vegetarian, Tyner explained at length the history and destiny of The Tooker, and of Tooker Ciity and of his career in recycling. He spoke in a clipped, shrill voice, almost birdlike at times, and taut like the wires he recycled from Ma Bell.

He'd gone down this path because in 1966 his aunt had died. She'd been an interior decorator in Gary, Indiana, and Tyner descended with a bunch of other relatives to plunder her estate. He was struck by the sheer mass of material she had accumulated, much of it quite serviceable. A junk man was born. After that, it was learning and then fitting the pieces together. Until The Tooker was born, the completely recycled artifact.

Food? Food like telephone wires was everywhere. Carrots, you would be surprised at the useful amount of carrots thrown away at the market. Just a few carrots in the bunch get rotten or severely discolored and, why, they decide to throw the entire bunch away. Now, you can take those carrots, and perfectly good carrots they are, and take a knife and carefully cut away the rotten parts, and if you are a person who is sensitive to color and form, you can also cut away the discolored portions, and you will have some excellent eating and good nutrition. At least good nutrition for this nation. Have you noticed our peculiar standards for food? I go down to the Water Street market every day or so and I find food in the trash and people look upon me as peculiar, as if that food was somehow unsafe and inedible. Isn't it strange that people will accept vegetables drenched in malathion but back away from a vegetable barely soiled in a garbage bin? The amount of waste in this country. Take that garlic, SIXTY POUNDS OF GARLIC, and if you pick out the rotten clove here and there, perfectly good.

Tyner was a regular apostle of free food and scavenged meals. He had a reputation in the neighborhood for an awesome feat. Tyner ate roaches. He explained that they were extremely clean, always licking their feet, you know, that's why pesticide worked on them, and quite high in protein. The rotten produce, the vegetables, the brown rice, people could handle that. But the roaches, well, the roaches put Tyner in the first rank in American self-sufficiency. All this bug-eating, bicycle-riding, garbage-can-raiding, and recycling was but the launching pad for the big thing, The Tooker. And before The Tooker, all you gotta remember was,

CIGARETTE = SUGAR TIT.

It is quite simple.

CIGARETTE = SUGAR TIT.

To remedy this equation, The Tooker came into the world. [Americans are always gimme, gimme, gimme. No restraint, that is obvious. They consume so much, and they waste, my God, I am an expert on what they waste. I spend my days trying to salvage some of the metal and fiber and food and petroleum products like plastic, now you would think in our present straits, that people would not waste something precious like petroleum. But they do. [Gobble, Gobble, Gobble. Take this building, now I have to move, and I just moved in here eighteen months ago with my recycling center, and it is not easy for someone like myself to move. There is so much material, and my work. It is gimme, gimme, gimme.]

Now The Tooker remedies this. Have you ever noticed the way Americans smoke cigarettes? They draw down deeply and greedily, suck suck, suck. Where did this kind of behavior begin? Notice an infant nursing, the savage grab at the nipple, the violent sucking.

Sucking, sucking, sucking.

It is inherent in the words.

Notice.

CIGARETTE = SUGAR TIT.

Hear it in there?

CIGARETTE = SUGAR TIT.

Now with The Tooker, this is not possible. The design slows down the smoke, permitting the smoker to slowly and pleasurably inhale the smoke in useful quantities. This breaks one of the greedy sucking of cigarettes and teaches calm and moderation. Through use of The Tooker, Americans learn that more is not better, that gobbling is not good. They learn the proper perspective on the world, and from this they learn restraint. They reduce consumption and waste.

Look at this city and things thrown away and these people, and now I have to move and it is very difficult for someone like myself to move. It is very disruptive, and why should I have to move anyway? I am not wasting anything, I am not a drone, I have important work. Do you know why I have to move and take all my things and look for another place—it is very hard for someone like me, for a recycler to find a suitable place— do you know why I have to leave? So that people can have this space that want the floors sanded and polished and want the beamed ceiling sandblasted. I think it is perfectly adequate the way it is.

If only these people had The Tooker they would learn.

I don't think anyone should have to give up the space they are using as long as they are using it. I don't think people should be forced to move, to have their work disrupted.

A madman, correct? An eccentric, pointless person, spreading babble and The Tooker. Tyner, like Mexicans in Pilsen, like most Chicagoans most places most times, does not count. What does Tyner have to do with anything that matters, with stacking the wheat, moving the freight, warehousing the nation's bent and booming appetites. God, just look at him, skin and bone, a wraith of roach nurture. Move, Tyner, move dammit, for Dearborn Park, Chicago's next great neighborhood, for Printer's Row, Chicago's newest enclave of funk and hanging plants.

Tyner does not count, and he knows that.

⎡Sears Tower, as the world's tallest building, Sears Tower does count.

This much is obvious. This is the American city.

Large projects that require enormous capital count, regardless of return or lack of return.

Little things do not count, regardless of return.⎤

Anyway, Tyner is a goddamn nut. Listen. Listen to him there, arms flailing as he whips wire on yet another Tooker, working in a cloud of garlic.

Remember: CIGARETTE = SUGAR TIT. Did you know cigarettes were introduced into this country in 1890? Why? It was quite simple, and makes the need for The Tooker all that more obvious. The cigarette burned faster and permitted and encouraged deep inhalation of smoke and waste. No one saved the stub of a cigarette, they threw it away. They had saved cigars. And cigarettes went up in smoke almost instantly. The smoker needed more and more of them. Cigarettes teach greed, gobbling.

CIGARETTE = SUGAR TIT.

Do you realize that there are presently in this nation, 60,000,000 cigarette addicts? Now what do these 60,000,000 cigarette addicts do? They cause one-half of all fires statistically. And what is the consequence of this statistic? The destruction of American Independence, the dwindling of our most precious heritage, Freedom. What do we endure because of this greedy sucking of air by cigarette addicts? High insurance rates, which crush cheap living quarters for working people. And what do these insurance companies demand to protect themselves from the addicts that finance their very prosperity? BUILDING CODES.

Building codes that no one can follow, that drive persons such as myself out of quarters like my recycling center here and

108

5 Fire

In the 1920s, the Gads Hill settlement house interviewed residents of Pilsen. The old people talked of work and of housing and of building Chicago. They tried to get the past down right and the past came down as movement.

> When did the railroad come through of there? Soon
> enough, soon enough, but a tough time they had a movin'
> us off their land. I remember wan family, squatters like the
> rest of us, wouldn't and the tracks bein' laid closter and
> closter to thim each day, till finally wan dark mornin' early
> as they was havin' their wee breakfast, there came a scalp
> raisin' toot from the ingine that stud with its head fairly
> poked in their windy—Sure, they up and moved thin!
> —Gads Hill memoir

From the beginning the way had been plain, and the way was movement and commerce and yet more movement.

The bog's first settler was a black man, DuSable. He sold iron for fur. Others came and traded with the Indians, followed the ups and downs of the market for pelts. When wolf packs drifted near, the little community hunted wolves. For the first decade of the 19th century this Chicago drifted in a sea of grass. Then one August morning in 1812, war between Britain and the United States forced the abandonment of the place. Five hundred Potawatomi warriors waited in the grass. They killed twenty-six soldiers, two women and twelve children. Others they tortured down by the Lake. They burned the fort. The survivors fled into the prairie, the dead lay unburied.

Movement and commerce.

109

By the 1830s, the once mighty Potawatomis had been raked by various diseases, nibbled to death by treaties, and were ripe for export. The beaver were gone. Chicago had exhausted its first cut off the hinterland. The tribe, known as "People of the Place of the Fire," trekked west to the cage of treaty rights.

> They assembled at the council house, near where the Lake House now stands, on the north side of the river. All were entirely naked except for a strip of cloth around the loins. Their bodies were covered all over with a great variety of brilliant paints. . . .
> The long coarse black hair was gathered into a profusion of hawk's and eagle's feathers. . . .
> They advanced not with a regular march, but a continued dance. . . .
>
> —John Dean Caton, 1935

Twelve months later Fort Dearborn closed, Chicago's first economic dud, a trailblazer for all the Sears Towers that would emulate it by always looking backward instead of forward. The Potawatomis were felled by progress like all the other people who would be successively evicted from the spot as changes in the means of production translated them from labor to human junk.

Eviction is part and parcel of residence in Chicago. The Potawatomis were distinctive in being the first to discover that they ran a distant second to commerce. Location created the city and the city became a function of the location. All else, man and beast, house and church, mansion and slum were happenstances wedged between the pathways of goods. Chicago did not set out to be anybody's home, but everybody's factory.

> There can be no two places in the world more completely thoroughfares than this place and Buffalo. They are the two correspondent valves that open and shut all the time,

as the life blood rushes from the east to the west, and back
again from the west to the east.

—Margaret Fuller, 1843

   The bog held a few hundred people in 1830. By the 1880s it
was the fifth or sixth largest cluster of people on the globe. Why
did so many human beings crowd onto a bog? Later generations
would ponder the merits of founding fathers or plumb the wisdom of capitalism. The view in the 1830s was clearer. Geologist
Henry Schoolcraft. " . . . To the ordinary advantages of a
marketing town," he argued, "it must, hereafter, add that of a
depot for inland commerce, between the northern and southern
sections of the Union, and a great thoroughfare for strangers,
merchants and travelers."
   CLIMB! all the observers roared, and Chicago complied with
a growth that became the benchmark in the industrial world.

   When the river was crooked, they made it straight. When it
   fouled their drinking water by flowing north into lake
   Michigan, they dug their famous drainage canal and com-
   pelled it to run south into the Mississippi and Gulf of
   Mexico. When the Lake trespassed on Lincoln Park, they
   drove it back with a marvelous sea wall of masonry and
   marble. . . . Nothing that either man or nature can do,
   apparently can check the growth of this city that has spread
   back from the Lake like a prairie fire, until its great bulk
   covers nearly two hundred miles of Illinois.
                        —Newton Dent, *Munsey's Magazine,* 1907

Climb.
   This idea called the city rested on the natural system. Chicago
was a manmade transformer of the vast forests, the thick prairie
sods, the fisheries, deep mineral beds, mines of coal, millions of
domestic animals. The city was not on a hill, erected as an ideal
for striving humans everywhere. The city was on a bog and its

only idea for itself and for its people was the process of consumption, movement and spent resources. Chicago called for no philosophers, but for strong backs and cunning engineers. It became the basic American city, a place never burdened by a higher mission than its appetites.

Chicago's opportunity was to be this thing, the industrial city in all its purity and ferocity. There was no other intention and there was no other result. Later generations of pork kings and traction giants would attempt to graft an opera house here and art gallery there to clothe and hide the appetite of the marketplace.

First came the canal. Humans in the 1820s and 30s argued ditch over railroad because any man could put a boat in a ditch but only the rich could put an iron horse on the rails. After much delay, a ninety-seven mile link between the Mississippi and the Great Lakes was finished in 1848. Bridgeport, three miles out of town, became the first Chicago neighborhood, a shantytown thrown up for the canal's Irish laborers. Joined with the Erie finished in 1825, the new ditch completed an arc of commerce from Manhattan to New Orleans and beyond.

A hundred people in 1830. Four thousands residents in 1840. By 1843, 700 vessels cleared the harbor. With the canal in the air, there was speculation on the ground.

> Emigrants coming almost everyday in wagons of various forms and in many instances families were living in their covered wagons while arrangements were made for putting up shelter for them. It was no uncommon thing for a house such as would answer for the purpose for the time being to be put up in a few days.
>
> —Charles Butler, 1830s

> . . . off we go ashore and walk through the busy little town,
> busy even then, people hurry to and fro, frame buildings
> going up, board sidewalks going down, new hotels, new
> churches, new theaters, everything new. Saw and
> hammer—saw! saw! bang! bang!
> —Joseph Jefferson, Sr., Actor, 1838

In the year 1835, eighty percent of the population had been resident less than twelve months.

The canal was something more than a ninety-seven mile chute of water. As the *Niles Register* had commented when the idea was floated in 1814, "What a route! How stupendous the idea! . . . . If it should ever take place . . . the Territory will become the seat of an immense commerce and a market for the commodities of all regions." No one misunderstood the canal, not the expectant hundreds hammering and sawing in the thirties, not the hopeful thousands perched on the edge of the boom when the locks opened in 1848.

> The city is situated on both sides of the Chicago River, a
> sluggish slimy stream too lazy to clean itself, and on both
> sides of its north and south branches, upon a level piece of
> ground, half dry and half wet. Real estate agents were
> mapping out the surrounding territory for ten to fifteen
> miles in the interior, giving fancy names to future avenues,
> streets, squares and parks.
> —John Lew Peyton, 1848

The canal changed the geography of the continent. The lumber, grain, and meat of the countryside now came faster to Chicago. This increase in speed and volume fed a new level of growth. At first glance, it looks so idyllic, the Irish workers squatting at Bridgeport on the new ditch, the men on the towpaths singing and prodding the mules forward at a walk. But the first glance is deceiving. The canal upped the tempo.

For centuries, men had built shelter by sinking heavy posts to support heavy beams. Such structures took a long time to put up and a long time to fall down. (The canal, coupled with new steam-driven saws and cheap factory nails, prompted people to build differently.) The new method, called balloon construction, was first used in St. Mary's church in 1833. A frame was swiftly put up of 2 x 4s and 2 x 6s held together with nails. Boards were slapped on this fragile looking frame. The system worked. Soon housing contracts called for completion within a week. The canal was forcing new kinds of buildings to be built. "If it had not been for the knowledge of the balloon frame," concluded the New York *Tribune* in 1855, "Chicago and San Francisco would never have arisen, as they did, from little villages to great cities in a single year."

Humans sprawled on both sides of the Chicago River seeking to divine in which direction the energy would explode. Southsiders and northsiders warred over bridges, each fearing such links would channel wealth away from them. When the city council voted to tear down one rickety bridge to the north in 1839, southsiders, who needed no bridges, arose before dawn and had at the span with axes. By 1836, the first suburban house went up; within twenty years, the word suburb was part of the language. The energy of the canal kept pushing against the city for new openings. By 1850, Mayor Long John Wentworth argued that the cops must be made to live in Chicago's scattered districts if the people were to be tamed.

Cyrus McCormick brought his reaper works from Virginia in 1847. The next year the city shipped 2,000,000 bushels of wheat, up from 700,000 in 1843.

The very things which concentrated the wheat, concentrated people and made for epidemics, traffic congestion, and filth. Buildings hugged the river and its branches, knifing off at odd angles along old Indian trails. Privies dotted the city and the urine and feces dribbled and gushed into the river and lake. Drinking water came from a wooden pipe snaked out on the lake bottom. When the waste met the drink, people died. Cholera dragged many each year to fresh, wet graves. Haze hung from the wood fires. Teamsters cursed and struggled through the crowded streets. The canal had made a new world. A small investment in time and money had channeled a torrent onto the bog. People responded. Chicago ballooned.

The city exploding with growth decked itself out with the look of a village. Greek Revival architecture with its columns, white paint and green shutters became the dominant style of the canal Chicago. The booming port took the motto of city in the garden. Buildings were not tall, homes were surrounded by yards. Trees struggled everywhere. It was as if having looked upon what they had wrought, these early Chicagoans then re-treated into a fantasy. Their city would be a town, their downtown houses would be right off a New England village green. While the city flexed and muscled itself into new patterns and new dimensions, the architecture visually promised the security of other places and other times. The effort failed.

The railroad came. There was not a single mile of track in 1848. Chicago was the railroad center of the West by 1854. First there was a thirty mile spur to Elgin with the locomotive Pioneer chugging down the new rails. By 1855, 3000 miles of track converged on the city, ten trunk lines and eleven branches snorted through the green shuttered districts. Each and every day ninety six trains came to town. Chicago reached out to the Mississippi at sixteen points. On the eve of the Civil War the city pastured 820 locomotives, 1500 cars, and punched fares for 65,000,000. The canal town of 1847 held 16,000 people and hosted a convention for 20,000. Thirteen years later, 100,000 camped by the Lake, toiled at 500 factories, and handled the freight of fifteen railroads.

The iron horse shoved the mules aside; the steam powered city devoured the canal town. The city in the garden disappeared in this change. As more and more commerce flourished downtown, tall buildings appeared. Then came the horse drawn streetcars in 1850. Within six years, eighteen lines made 400 trips per day. A horse ambles along about twice as fast as a man. This meant that residential space doubled since people could live twice as far from work and still get there in the same amount of time. Before the streetcar the rich and the poor had been forced to live together. Packing king Alexander Clybourne lived next to his stinking slaughterhouse. Mayor William Butler Ogden, a real estate wizard, went home each night to a mansion surrounded by shanties. On the bog of Chicago, money bought dry ground, not segregation by income. With the streetcar this ended. Those with money could afford longer commutes; those who could not got left behind.

These are the things that design cities: canals, oats in a horse's belly, lumps of coal. Architects sit at drafting tables dreaming New Romes, imagining facades, thinking they design the city. A horse clomps by on the cobblestone street, there under the gaslight. A train whistles in the yards. The architect does not notice. He continues to ink in a cornice.

The port of 1844 swallows 440,000 tons of shipping, the port of 1869, 3,000,000. McCormick's reapers are out past the city's haze mowing flat the Red River of the north. The locomotives drag back 60,000,000 bushels, the seventeen giant elevators lining the river suck and spew cascades of grain.

The buffalo and prairie wolves have followed the Potawatomi into exile. Hogs, cattle, sheep follow in their wake cropping the land. At first the domestic animals walked to market, a cheap way to haul corn and grass to town. Christmas Day, 1865, the Union Stockyards open for business; the pens cover a square mile, hold 20,000 steers, 75,000 pigs, 20,000 sheep. Nine railroads build spurs to the sharp blades and din of squeals, bellows, roars. Before, meat walked. Now pork, beef, mutton moves at the velocity of steam. Now the grass of the mid-continent arrives in Chicago by express. The refrigerator car appears in 1869. The range of the carnage expands.

Climb.

One summer day in 1869, three thousand four hundred immigrants land at Chicago. Another day, 300 vessels make port in twelve hours. Drawbridges on the river go up and down as boats pass at a rate of two per minute. On the South Branch at Pilsen a lumber industry emerges and looks to the forests of northern Minnesota, Wisconsin, Michigan. Along the bank Czech woodworkers sharpen their tools. In 1867, a billion and a half board feet of lumber reach their skilled hands. Pilsen holds the largest concentration of lumber on earth. Pilsen needs wood, wood, and more wood. To the north, boys barely men go off to the winter lumber camps; to the north the spring rise in the rivers carries logjams, men hopping from log to log, men twirling the slick bark beneath their feet, sometimes falling to their deaths in the cold waters and crush of wood. Pilsen needs wood, needs clean grain, whorl, and burl. Keep cutting, keep chopping. The upper Midwest is cut flat to the ground. It passes into the history books as a sea of stumps called the cutover region. The lumber barons move west.

This crude city of steam power would forever haunt the people by the lake shore. Slight alterations in structure, a canal dug by hand, had so radically altered the things discussed under the heading of the economy, the community, the work. Change had swept over the natural system of bog and lake and river with a speed humans could barely comprehend. It had all been so swift, so noisy, so dirty—and yet so easy.

Later generations would discover the poor, then the slums, then the demons of planning and urban renewal, and they would find their city an intractable and unwieldy place. As petroleum washed over the bog in the twentieth century and the rate of consumption skyrocketed and the blaze of energy grew hotter and hotter and the movement of humans and materials approached new theoretical velocities, a new characteristic of the place would be noticed. As more and more was poured on the land, more and more structures were necessary to contain the crush of goods and humans and to channel them, and everything slowed down, clogged, and the dream that was to explode into the modern age froze instead. But not in the steam city, no not there. That one could be grappled with, that one gave birth to the Chicago slogan: I will.

George Pullman came to the Chicago of 1850 to make his fortune. He found this city built on a bog, mired in its own muck. The city council voted to raise the roadbeds with river sludge and thus put transportation on high dry ground. Streets rose up four to seven feet, leaving the buildings behind and below. For cottage owners and small property holders, this was of little consequence. The first floor suddenly became the basement. But for businessmen, the money-making first floor sank from view and from profit. Pullman fixed that. Line up hundreds of men with hundreds of screw jacks and blow a whistle. Each blast of sound and the jacks were spun a revolution. Downtown emerged, building by building, from the bog. It was that simple, that easy. The structure was that flexible.

Then there was the consequence of the new horse drawn streetcars. People moved with the new networks and suddenly many houses seemed to be in the wrong place. The rich—the barons of pork, lumber and wheat, and retail goods—built places south of the Loop at Twenty-Second and Indiana, Prairie, Calumet, and South Park. Boat traffic kept the draw-bridges up so much that many were leery of a north side commute across the river. Those of lesser fortune just packed up home and moved.

> From rapid growth of the city some of the edifices are rendered unsuitable for what they originally intended; this has given rise to the extraordinary practice of house moving for which this city is so famous. No sooner is a better house wanted in any given location than the old erection is put upon wheels or roller and drawn off to a more suburban site. . . .
>
> —two Scots, 1869

People would sit at windows sipping tea and perusing a periodical while riding their home down the avenues.

The best demonstration of the vitality and resources came in October 1871. Chicago burnt to the ground. Nothing but ash and rubble for three and three-quarters square miles in the urban heart. The business district, the swank hotels all gone. A hundred thousand humans were homeless, 300 were dead and $200,000,000 worth of structure was rendered smoke and heat and char. Chicago in a brief flicker of flame changed from the wonder of the world to the disaster of the world.

Much was spared. The stockyards survived untouched along with 75% of the grain elevators, 80% of the lumberyards, and 600 factories. The railroads, the canal and the inherent strength of the location were unchanged and unscathed. The flames licked the shacks of the poor and the emporiums of the merchants but spared channels and structures that poured resources into the city. And the men who made fortunes on the spot realized the spot was not destroyed but rather made available for radical development.⟩

"Chicago," explained local capitalist Stephen Wright on the morning after the fire, "will have more men, more money, more business within five years than she would have had without the fire." The canal city remnants had perished, now the steam city of the railroads could emerge without obstacles. Cyrus McCormick lost a $2,000,000 plant. Within 90 days, he was turning out reapers at a new plant on Western Avenue. Potter Palmer, a merchant king, lost everything. He quickly obtained a $2,000,000 loan from an eastern insurance company, at the time the largest single loan ever made to an individual. Six weeks after the fire, 318 new buildings were going up, a combined frontage of three and a half miles. Not nearly enough architects for the task—old blueprints were taken from smoke blackened safes and pressed into use.

Retail patterns were shifted from an east-west axis to a north-south axis. A new appetite for stone and brick became evident as the city realized flimsy structures could not cope with such a concentration of humans and materials. A fire district of brick first encompassed downtown and then with the years spread out over the metropolis. Reporters attempting to cover the fire's origins in an Irishwoman's barn, discovered another Chicago of filth and poverty at a spot near Pilsen, a kind of dark continent heretofore unsuspected.

The People of the Fire were long gone, the arrow surrendered to the canal, the ditch in turn retired as a primary force by the locomotive. The city disguised in green shutters and Greek Revival as a community, a bloated New England village, now unmasked as a colossal pump draining the region of storages, of soil, timber, fiber, animal flesh and mineral. The city now revealed as a process as much as a place, an open ended smithy that consumed and transformed and incidentally housed humans between rails and forges. Burn it to the ground and it springs back, bigger, stronger, yet fuller of social consequence. For a nation in which the market was becoming everything, for which the market was becoming not the way to some undefined good life but the life itself, Chicago approached the new national essence.

The locomotive is coming through the window.

Climb.

6 Spiral Stair Case

Dick ripped the roof off but nobody was home. The six flat in Pilsen had sprung into being with the boom of the postfire city. Sunk in the area around the International Harvester plant of Cyrus McCormick on 19th and Peoria, the pile of apartments had sheltered blue collar generations. Now all was empty, and a look down from the roof revealed a skeleton of main beams, exterior walls, and little else. A claw-legged bathtub sat forlornly on a landing.

It was all part of a project funded with VICI (Ventures in Community Improvement) money to teach local Mexicans the trade of carpentry and to provide good subsidized housing as a bonus. While Tom the architect struggled across the street, turning an old dump into a bit of inner-city charm, and while the local housing czar acquired his dozens of buildings against the day when the neighborhood went middle class, the VICI project competed for the available units and slowly turned old holes into attractive apartments. Dick was a journeyman who trained the apprentice carpenters in the craft. Clambering around the roof with a half dozen of them, he taught how to make things from wood, all this with the union's grudged blessings which were a concession to minority demands for union slots.

Dick had the building trades bred in his bones, and he had been tugged into Pilsen by ties of blood or history or both. Chicago is the American industrial city, and it sometimes beckons back the sons and grandsons, daughters and grand-daughters of the workers who build such places. They walk among the ruins of nineteenth-century might. Tom the architect, scheming his hand-finished home in Pilsen, was Chicago-born, and for all his attraction to the blue skies of Mexico, he was still in Chicago in the rotting remnants of one of the metropolis' working class districts. Then there was Bob, an organizer in his twenties who oversaw the VICI project that placed Dick on the roof, riping rotten boards. Bob's grandfather had baked bread in Pilsen for decades, spending the early morning hours before the searing ovens. A bunch of seminarians who had left the Church of Rome had landed in Pilsen ten years ago; they found the place poor enough for what apparently was to be a life of Christian witness to the grind of the big city on the people who work the big city. Dick? Well, Dick's grandfather had been a carpenter who knew how to build spiral staircases, and here he was at about age 30, plying the family trade in the former world center for lumber. Pilsen was homecoming for anyone whose people had ever worked with their hands and carried lunch pails.

The pull was strong, at least had been strong. The pull had been work. A constant going back and forth from the corn counties to the mills, making the dollar. Just as the Mexicans now slipped up north for the wages and then dreamed of going back, so had generations of Americans from the districts and states surrounding Chicago.

Things would go on, though, in a dim kind of way until the better thing would eventuate, and Carrie would be rewarded for coming and toiling in the city. . . .

In 1889, Chicago had the peculiar qualifications of growth which made such adventuresome pilgrimages even on the part of young girls plausible. Its many and growing commercial opportunities gave it widespread fame, which made of it a giant magnet, drawing to itself from all quarters, the hopeful and the hopeless. . . .

She walked east along Van Buren Street. . . . She
walked bravely forward, led by an honest desire to find
employment and delayed at every step by the interest of the
unfolding scene, and a sense of helplessness amid so much
evidence of power and force which she did not understand.
These vast buildings, what were they. These strange ener-
gies and huge interests, for what purposes were they there?
She could have understood the meaning of a little stone-
cutter's yard at Columbus City, carving little pieces of
marble for individual use, but when the yards of some huge
stone corporation came into view, filled with spur tracks
and flat cars, transpierced by docks from the river and
traversed overhead by immense trundling cranes of wood
and steel, it lost all significance in her little world.
                    —Theodore Dreiser, *Sister Carrie*

Now, generations after the city of mule and horse and locomotive, and in the midst of the decline of the city of coal and
oil, many came to examine the remains. Like ancient Roman
diviners, they scanned the entrails of the industrial explosion
trying to figure out what had happened and what remedy was
possible for this great fall. The hopes of 1889, when Sister
Carrie had wandered in awe watching the structures grow from
the mucky ground, were now the derelicts to be bulldozed, or in
the case of Dick's six flat, to be rehabilitated for one more
generation of immigrants.

 Originally they thought a wall must be taken out there, a
stairway repaired here, a floor redone, a bathroom retiled. But
the rot was much deeper. They ripped and sorted and ripped
again and were left with a skeleton: exterior walls of brick and
the basic beams of the interior. All else was beyond salvage. But
what better place to teach carpentry? The crew was starting
from scratch. They were doing it right, they were following
code, and that meant cutting deep, right down to the bone. This

time they were going to build the city properly, or at least build one six flat properly.

Dick did things properly. He carried in his head whole systems of the right way. He was a master carpenter and he wanted to impart to his apprentices skills they would seldom use in the prefab world of modern construction.

Dick, besides his carpenters' Union card, carried one for IWW.

Carpentry and the Industrial Workers of the World. Spiral staircase and Solidarity Forever. Like so many humans, Dick carried vital notions to get him through the workday. But his notions, his systems, were in ruins. Carpentry was for apprentices, prefab industrial construction for journeymen. The spiral staircase had gone away and left staple guns. The I.W.W., the one big industrial Union that meant something important, was a living ghost. Big Bill Haywood's ashes were in the Kremlin, and no more mill girls carried the sign seen at Lawrence in 1912, "We want some bread and roses, too."

He ate lunch at an old mom-and-pop store half a block from the six flat. The place didn't stock much but it made good sandwiches. An old couple ran it. The daughter took the order, ham on rye mustard lettuce tomato no onion—and he made it. He was getting close to eighty, but with a full head of white hair and massive eyebrows like those of John L. Lewis. There were no secrets here, no microwave shortcuts. Ask for a sandwich and they took two slices of bread and started throwing cold cuts and mustard around. Get a bag of chips, a coke, and call it lunch. Out on the curb, Dick talks. About the apprentices, about the trade unions, about carpentry, about the Wobblies.

New machines, ever replacing less productive ones, wipe out whole trades and plunge new bodies of workers into the ever growing army of tradeless, hopeless employed. . . .

A *dead line* has been drawn, and an age limit established,
to cross which, in this world of monopolized opportunities,
means condemnation to industrial death. . . .

The worker, wholly separated from the land and the tools,
with his skill of craftsmanship rendered useless, is sunk in
the uniform mass of wage slaves.

—I.W.W. Manifesto, adopted at Chicago,
January 2, 3, and 4, 1905

Sitting on a stoop munching his sandwich, Dicks says the
apprentices are all right, but it is hard to convince them of the
need for good work, for doing it right, for building things true.
Some of them balk at real work, at doing everything from
scratch. He speaks quietly, almost in a monotone, with care and
some caution, making sure he gets it just right. They don't
understand, he explains, that you have to know all this, that the
people in the Union will test them to get their card as journeymen and if they do not know it they will flunk. Because the
others will know it, the others will have been trained properly.
It is all cut and dried. The Union still has standards even if the
construction industry increasingly does not. You have to get it
right.

The six flat is all right. Plumb doorways, sound floors, good
roof, eventually even a new cornice circling the structure. When
was the last time anyone in Chicago did a cornice? The cornice
is important as an idea and as an action, just like the spiral
staircase. In the city of Chicago, with aging buildings shoe-
horned between the pathways carved by technologies and the
loot of mid continent, there are few levers available that shift
the structure, the neighborhood, the urban mass from here to
there. There are planners, but no believable plan on the street,
no plan a man can put his shoulder to, no craft to be pursued.
Yet the city is full of people, always a minority, perhaps now a

dwindling minority, dedicated to craft, to true lines, sharp tools, proper procedures, and sound work. They are seemingly impervious to talk of gray collar, blue collar, white collar, information explosions—all things proffered as escapes from hard work, straight lines, sharp tools. Standards. They are like spiral staircases and Wobblies. A refusal to give in, a memory of a different dream.

Dick feeds on both. His grandfather could make a spiral staircase. It was a matter of templates, of a basic pattern adjusted to the circumstances of the structure. Most carpenters could never make a spiral staircase. It was always a supreme test. For humans, the design goes way back. Some nineteenth century students of architecture believed the first such staircase was the Tower of Babel around 6000 years ago.

> And they said one to another, Go to, let us make brick and burn them thoroughly. And they had brick for stone, and slime had they for mortar.
>
> And they said, Go to, let us build us a city and a tower, whose top *may reach* unto heaven; and let us make a name, lest we be scattered abroad upon the face of the whole earth. . . .
>
> And the Lord said, Behold, the people is one, and they have all one language; and this they begin to do: and now nothing will be restrained from them, which they have imagined to do.
>
> Go to, let us go down, and there confound their language, that they may not understand one another's speech.
>
> —Genesis, 11:3-7

After that it showed up in military towers, and in medieval Europe in castle walls. Often, the spiral circled to the left. Some have argued that this is because the average right-handed man climbing such a staircase would cling to the central column with his right hand, his sword hand, thus hindering his assault. Defenders coming from above would have their sword hands free. From the castles of war the spiral went to palaces of peace, finally entering the new homes of wealthy Renaissance merchants, where it became the centerpiece of the house, a symbol of castle strength and kingly wealth in the bourgeois home. For the carpenter, it remained a touchstone of craft. A matter of templates, adjustment, a thing of beauty as well as function. A thing which may have begun in the first human high technology solution and the first human high technology disaster. A stairway to paradise that led to babble.

The Wobblies were an attempt to confound the barriers of languages and divisions of craft. They offered one big union as the stairway to paradise. While Joe Hill decried pie in the sky, the Wobbly leader Father Thomas J. Hagerty drew one big pie here on earth. In the center was the president of the union surrounded by the General Administration. Then an inner circle of administrators. Finally, the slices of the departments—Manufacture, Public Service, Distribution, Food Stuffs, Agriculture, Mining, Transportation, and Building.

One obligation for all.
A union man once and in one industry, a
union man always and in all industries.
Universal transfers.
Universal emblem.
All workers of one industry in one union;
all unions of workers in one big labor
alliance the world over.

—*Voice of Labor,* 1905

(All of these workers faced the future with an overpowering idea stated in simple language: "the working class and the employing class have nothing in common. There can be no peace so long as hunger and want are found among millions of working people and the few, who make up the employing class, have all the good things of life.")

In the shambles of the modern day AFL-CIO, of the Teamsters and the UAW, this seems to be an idea as simple and true as the spiral staircase. A clean cut thing. The trick with the IWW, as with the spiral staircase, is to keep the damn things from sliding into lore, into a toy box of history where ideas are handled with affection because of their irrelevance.

The Reds, the Left, love to talk of kicking things into the dust bin of history, a junkyard of the mind. But Americans have prepared an even meaner fate, where the idea is picked clean and given a new coat of paint and described as premature or excessive or a symptom of a real wrong but distorted so as to be no remedy. Simplistic, ye gods, simplistic. Into this toy box goes Shays Rebellion, the communitarian movement, anarchism, populism, Sockless Jerry Simpson, worker movements of Andrew Jackson's America, a fistful of surviving speeches by native chiefs, Henry Adams' *Letter to Teachers of American History,* W.E.B. DuBois, and Big Bill Haywood picking up a board at 10 A.M. June 27, 1905 at Brand's Chicago Hall and banging the meeting to order, addressing the throng that would become the IWW, as "Fellow Workers."

(The Industrial Workers is organized not to conciliate but to fight the capitalist class. . . . The capitalists own the tools they do not use and the workers use the tools they do not own.)

—Eugene V. Debs, Grand Central
Palace, New York, December 10, 1905

Dick eats his sandwich on the stoop of the quiet, tree-lined street. Two miles away, maybe a little less, Sears Tower looms, a black hulk stuffed with typewriters and computers processing orders to buy and orders to sell. It isn't easy for him to keep his hammer in his hand and his brain focused on some logic beyond fringe benefits. The things he teaches the young Mexican apprentices about tools and the boards have all gone by the boards because of the new tools. Dick is cranking out complete carpenters for a world which grudgingly uses them for piece work on modular housing schemes. In his pocket is his IWW union book, stamped and paid up. In his head all the knowledge needed to turn a tree into a house.

He holds fast to the dream, looks through the quiet street under the doomed elms to the last IWW action. Downstate, down in central Illinois. It was something. Old guys came out, guys sixty, seventy, retired now in Florida, pensioned. Old working stiffs.

'Meet Me In the Jungle Louie'
(tune: Meet Me in St. Louis, Louie)

Louie was out of a job,
Louie was dead on the hog;
He looked all around,
But no job could be found.
So he had to go home and sit down.
A note on the table he spied,
He read it just once and he cried,
It read: 'Louie, dear, get the hell out of here
Your board bill is now overdue.'

Chorus:

Meet me in the jungle, Louie
Meet me over there
Don't tell me the slaves are eating
Anywhere else but there;

We will each one be a booster
To catch a big fat rooster;
So meet me in the jungle, Louie
Meet me over there.

These guys had seen it all, not theorists or armchair revo-
lutionaries, I haven't got much time for academics. We were
having a picket, a peaceful show of support. And they show up,
from all over, just like the old days when they would ride the
freights to wherever they were needed. They came with pipes
and boards and guns. We had to say cool it, it's not like that.

Hymn of Hate

For Homestead and for Chicago, Coeur D'Alene and
   Telluride,
For your bloody shambles at Ludlow, where the women
   and babies died,
For our heroes you hanged on gallows high to fill your
   slaves with awe,
While your judges stood in a sable row and croaked, 'Thus
   saith the law.'
For all of the wrongs we have suffered from you and for
   each of the wrongs we hate,
With a hate that is black as the deepest pit, that is steadfast
   and sure as fate,
We hate you with hand and heart and head and body and
   mind and brain.

—Harry "Haywire Mac" McClintock,
Solidarity, January 1, 1916

Lunch is over.

Back to the roof and the apprentices and the six flat that is
being salvaged and restored. When all is done, the apartments
will rent for less than comparable ones in the area, and
some Mexicans will have been added to the rolls of the car-

penters' union. These are both good things. The building will look good and be sound. One more good thing. How can one object to this process? How can one criticize this VICI project? In the entire city of Chicago, this VICI project, six apartments and a fistful of apprentices, is the showplace. The Mayor says, Here, look at this one, it works. For those fretting over bad housing in Chicago, over job retraining in Chicago, Here, look at this one, it works.

The fire worked better.

Better?

A few weeks after the Great Chicago Fire, three-and-a-half miles of frontage went up, going up stone where there had been wood, getting better. All eastern money was anxious to buy in. The fire did not destroy Chicago, it shoved the canal city aside and gave the railroad city a clear shot at a thing called the future. But now the city was back in the muck. A VICI project crawls along for a year or two to provide six apartments at a liveable rent and train a half dozen to a dozen apprentices.

After the fire they built spiral staircases in Chicago.

After the fire in Brand's Hall, the IWW was born in Chicago.

After lunch, Dick went back to the roof, ripping out the rotten boards.

134

7 White City

Two hundred waiters popped 10,000 bottles of champagne, poured 35,000 quarts of beer. Outside the building on Wabash 15,000 Chicagoans yelled to get in. The bands struck up and herds of businessmen, whores, pimps, hugger muggers, louts, pickpockets and public servants danced to the music. A hundred cops chaperoned the event. The aldermen of the Loop and the adjacent red light district, Hinky Dink Mike Kenna and Bathhouse John Coughlin, looked at their creation, the 1st Ward's Annual Ball, 1907 version.

"Why," bragged Hinky Dink, "it's great! It's a lallapa-looza! . . . . Well, look at it! All the business houses are here, all the big people. All my friends are out. Chicago ain't no sissy town!" Kenna and Coughlin were crooked politicians and the people at the ball were either crooks or those who did business with crooks. They are part of the local color associated with turn of the century American cities, an era of bosses and bribes and champagne sipped from a harlot's slipper. They are concrete evidence that the city was overgrown. Like skyscrapers, settlement houses, and city plans, the two graft-ridden aldermen indicated that the cost of doing business in Chicago had gone up. They constituted a tax on the cost of moving goods and services.

This is the city that worked, that stacked all that wheat and slaughtered all those hogs. This city was overgrown, overdeveloped, overbuilt and beginning to show the inevitable signs of decay. As the city thrived on its railroads and commerce, it filled itself with structure and clogged itself with people. By

135

doing this it destroyed its major asset, its potential. In response
to its growth and congestion different groups attempted to sort
out an order. Hinky Dink and Bathhouse John and their
cohorts demanded bribes. Imagine the city's commercial life
flowing through a pipe; in this instance, politicians are valves.
For the valves to open and close properly bribes and wages were
called for.

Another effort to order this overdeveloped city came from
the academics and architects with their studies and their plans.
Daniel Burnham epitomized this view with his leadership during
the 1893 World's Fair and his 1909 Plan of Chicago. Both were
claims that the problems of the city could be overcome by
intelligent planning. In short, the problems were seen as temporary, not inherent. Burnham, a Chicago boy, was a friend of
Bathhouse John. His son Dan Jr. recalled,

> Bathhouse John was an old friend and admirer of my
> father. . . . When I came on the stage, he extended this
> friendship to me and for many years he helped me out with
> political favors. . . . Among his string of race horses, he
> had one named 'Dan Burnham' for my father. . . .

Whatever Burnham's thoughts on fixing the city, one should
remember his acts. In the late 1880s he moved his family to
Evanston because he "no longer could bear to have my children
run in the streets of Chicago." He bought an old farmhouse on
the lake.

The settlement houses suggested that the city suffered from a
moral lapse on the part of those who owned factories and those
who toiled in them. The reformers strove for little villages
emanating from the settlement houses. Neighborhoods would
be led by people with high ideals. New laws would clean up
housing, clean up factories, abolish drink, shelter women and
children.

The skyscraper was yet another response to the vitality Hinky Dink celebrated as a lallapalooza. Confronting the crush of bodies and buildings, the architects were forced upward in their solutions.

Between 1880 and 1890 the population grew from 502,298 to 1,098,570. Land in the Loop leapt in price from $130,000 in 1880 to $1,000,000 in 1890—this for a quarter acre. Marshall Field's emporium grossed $3,000,000 in 1872; ten years later the take was $24,000,000. George Pullman's first sleeping car found no takers; the $18,000 Palace Car was put in storage. In 1865, it was used for bringing Lincoln's body home to Illinois. By 1880 Pullman was plotting a model town on 4300 acres just south of the city. He powered his plant with the giant Corliss engine that had dazzled the world at the 1876 Centennial bash in Philadelphia. When it was first constructed there was not a single economic activity in the United States that required the full power of its output. After the celebration, it was dismantled and stored. In 1880, Pullman hired a train and hauled the Corliss west. In four short years, the steam monster had gone from curiosity to tool. In 1910, the engine was dismantled again and sold for scrap. Too small.

The stockyards killed 3,000,000 hogs in 1872, 5,000,000 in 1882, 7,000,000 in 1892. This killing ground was not a local matter. The British Empire stormed into the Sudan of 1883 fueled by 740,000 pounds of canned Chicago beef. A year later, the desert army swallowed 2,500,000 pounds. By 1905, 75,000 men drew paychecks for murdering pigs, sheep and cows. Their wages supported the surrounding district of 250,000. That year, 17,000,000 animals rode the rails to Chicago and left town as $500,000,000 worth of meat, hides and glue.

Growth seemed easy, effortless and almost unconscious. But in the health and vitality of Chicago were the elements later generations would identify as blight, stagnation, dispersal and strangulation. As the city grew so did its problems, and with the new size proposed solutions loomed ever more gigantic.

Imagine the simple acts of daily life. A man gets up, empties his bowels, travels to work, makes something, returns home. Say it is 1875 and the man lives in a shanty, relieves himself in a privy, walks to work, toils in a factory with 100 other hands, walks home. Now retouch this scene with progress. The shanty gives way to an apartment building, the privy to a flush toilet and sewage system, the walk to a streetcar. The factory booms to a thousand men, the return home is also by rail. This was the shift underway in Chicago in the late nineteenth century. Look closely at the changes. The shanty is toppled easily for the apartment building. The privy was effective with a small population, but as numbers grew gave way to an expensive sewage system that continually needs enlargement. The street car brings more and more people to the Loop. They jam together and the transportation system that was to increase the speed of travel begins to lose speed as sheer numbers drag it down. The factory must build a new huge plant for all its employees. And so on.

Finally, the city becomes so built, the streets so clogged, the air and water so dirty, the taxes to support the density so high that some begin to leave. Factories move to the suburban belt where there is still space. This continues until the condition of the city becomes the condition of the region. When the Midwest is built and developed, indeed overdeveloped in the sense that it must have imports to survive, industries move on to new areas which are undeveloped. In the twentieth century this has taken them to the West and the South.

All these changes were underway at the turn of the century when Chicago was booming, and when the urban crisis of stagnation that would seize attention a half century later was unthought and unimagined. [The city had never really cared much for its inhabitants, stuffing them willy nilly between railroads and factories. But, it also seemed blind to its own fate, and worshipped signs of the problem as solutions.⟩

This is something very simple, yet something that must be reckoned with. (Industrial cities grow by diminishing their resource base and by choking their commerce with people and buildings. For the industrial city success is a form of slow suicide. ⟩

Chicago educator Francis Parker remarked at the turn of the century that "Chicago has the bones of a giant. . . . " Tinkering with these bones, the advantages of the geographical setting, led to an early exit of industry from the city. Federal money dredged Calumet Harbor south of the city in 1869, the first boat docking in 1870. Steel mills descended, Pullman planted his model town nearby. By 1883 the Illinois Central hammered a branch to the new district. Four years later a belt railroad arced for thirty five miles around the city. This iron necklace invented Elgin, Aurora, Joliet, Chicago Heights, and later Gary. Between 1910 and 1916, the population stagnated at 1,000,000 in a four miles radius from State and Madison in the Loop. From four to seven miles out human numbers grew from 460,000 to 1,076,000; seven to ten miles out the increase was from 180,000 to 320,000.

As early as 1890 businessmen assembled an intown industrial district to coax manufacturers to remain within the city. Covering a square mile north of the stockyards, the Central Manufacturing District provided industrialists with streets, railroad spurs, connected utilities, cheap loans and architects. These subsidies to industry slowed but did not stop the move beyond the city. For example, since the end of World War II,

172 industrial districts have been set up in the Chicago area, but only 23 of these in the city itself.

Transportation posed another problem. Horse cars gave way to cable cars which in turn were replaced by electric streetcars. By 1910, the system dumped 750,000 people a day into the Loop. The streets clogged with people and wagons. So they dug a subway for the goods.

"This is the latest Chicago idea," exclaimed a visiting journalist in 1907. "It is so new that few of the hurrying things in the downtown district have seen the wonderful railway system that is operating forty feet below the sidewalk. Yet it has already replaced seventy postal wagons and hundreds of drays. When it is in full swing it may go far toward clearing the streets of forty thousand turbulent teamsters and toward making Chicago the handiest city in the world."

When completed the system held 62 miles of tunnels, 117 locomotives and 3000 cars. The trains hauled freight, trash and garbage, the latter being dumped in barges for a thirteen mile voyage out into Lake. Contrary to the reporter's prophecy, Chicago did not become the handiest city in the world. Within thirty years the underground railroad gave way to what it had originally replaced: street traffic. Two things should be noted. One, the efforts to expedite traffic were crushed by the increased traffic the improvements brought. Two, all the improvements increased the fixed cost of doing business. A pathway forty feet beneath the city streets will always be more expensive than the city streets.

Another example of the same phenomenon was the enormity of the human waste, the ash, the chemicals, the offal, the trace metals, the thousand poisons excreted by the city. The Chicago that clustered humans, also clustered materials. By the late nineteenth century the materials were concentrating in amounts that killed the humans. Cholera, typhoid, typhus raked the population. This led to what the press hailed as the eighth wonder of the world.）

They created the Sanitary District in 1889 to rule the 185 square mile metropolis. This included the city proper and all its far flung satellites. The Chicago River's flow was reversed from the lake by dredging and locks, and it became a huge oxidizing ditch full of the waste. They dug sewers and ditches, and ran lines farther out into the Lake for clean water. When all the shovels were laid down, they had moved more dirt and rock than was required for the excavation of the Panama Canal.

This massive project was only the beginning, for the job would prove endless. Waste pumped backward into the Mississippi watershed would demand ever larger fortunes so that new cribs could be built in the Lake, new filtration plants on land. More and more water would have to be pumped from the Lake to propel the waste in the Chicago River on its way toward St. Louis. By the third quarter of the twentieth century the district would rule 860 square miles, and new projects would weigh in at eight and twelve billion dollars. The River would stink to the high heavens, the Lake would still be awash periodically with feces, and new poisons would come forth from the laboratories of the chemists to threaten the whole enterprise. The sheer mass of past solutions would impede future solutions.

As the bog was drained and became instead a morass of people, mortar, track and commerce, one new image seemed to liberate humans from a sense of being trapped and mired, an image that has continued to cast its spell to this day. Skyscraper. On the flatland by the flat lake rose a new and American canyonland, a vista described by Chicago born novelist Henry Fuller in his 1895 novel, *The Cliff Dwellers,*

Between the former site of old Fort Dearborn and the
present site of our newest Board of Trade there lies a
restricted yet tumultuous territory through which during
the course of the last fifty years, the rushing streams of
commerce have worn many a deep and rugged chasm. . . .
Each of these canyons is closed in by long frontage of
towering cliff, these soaring walls of brick and limestone
and granite rise higher and higher with each succeeding
year, according as the work of erosion goes onward. . . . Ten
years ago, the most rushing and irrepressible of the torrents
which devastate Chicago had not worn its bed to a greater
depth than that indicated by seven . . . 'stories.' This depth
has since increased to eight - to ten - to fourteen - to sixteen,
until some of the leading avenues of activity promise soon
to become little more than mere obscure trails, half lost
between the bases of perpendicular precipices.

(Humans felt freed by the sights infrequently glimpsed in their
trips to the summits of these structures. Now, after a lifetime in
Chicago, they could finally see Chicago.)

No one built more of these towers, twenty-seven in all, than
Burnham and Root, the architectural partnership of Daniel
Burnham and John Root. Before Root's death in 1892, the firm
designed $40,000,000 of buildings: 216 houses, 39 office
buildings, 23 railroad stations, 16 apartment buildings, 10
hotels, 9 schools, 7 warehouses, 5 stores, 3 hospitals. By 1900,
the firm had offices on both coasts and 180 employees.

In 1882 Burnham and Root put up a ten story tower, the Montauk Building, and from this stub the word skyscraper probably
came into the language. The facade was plain and each floor
above the first was identical. Henry Ericcson, a building con-
tractor, remembered arriving in Chicago from Germany and,
"Breathlessly, I turned west into Monroe Street where, beyond
Dearborn . . . I beheld the miracle being wrought. Facing south

on Monroe Street . . . the Montauk was rising to its third story. Seven stories more were to pierce the sky—the highest building so far undertaken. . . . "

The Montauk became famous because its look was so functional. The building lacked frills and ornament in a time that doted on both. "What Chartres was to the Gothic Cathedral," architect Thomas Tallmadge observed, "the Montauk Block was to the high commercial building."

This landmark was the creation of more than Burnham and Root. The building was designed in good part by the energy systems of the era, by the high land prices that forced commerce into vertical space, and by the penurious habits of two Boston capitalists who paid for it. Though towers of masonry design came into being in New York in the seventies, the telephone of 1876, the electric light of 1879, and later the electric elevator of 1889 made them work. Structural steel held them up as they reached ever higher. The elevators delivered people, the light chased darkness from the rooms, the telephone permitted people imprisoned in towers to talk with the outside world. The Montauk made use of what inventions were available and sensed the coming of others.

The brothers Peter and Shepherd Brooks were bears for detail. The Chicago school is credited with the maxim that form follows function, but perhaps this idea came from dealing with men like the brothers Brooks.

They wanted the building to be cheap, "a plain structure of face brick . . . with a flat roof." They dictated that the "building throughout is to be for use and not for ornament. Its beauty will be in its all-adaptation to its use." Cornices? "No projections on the building front (which catch dirt). . . . " Utilities? "The less plumbing, the less trouble. It should be concentrated as much as possible, all pipes to show and be accessible, including gas pipes.

It might be wise to put in wire for electric lights. It is not un-
common to do it in Boston now." Fancy tile surfaces? "Tile is
expensive and bothersome to keep clean, it is good for the floor
only—nowhere else." Lots of windows? " . . . Needless amount
of plate glass, the panes should be divided horizontally in
halves." Luminous colored glass? "Colored glass is mere nonsense, a passing fashion, inappropriate to a mercantile building
and worst of all, it obstructs light. Strike it out." Fancy urinals
and rest rooms? "What is the object in glass at the front of the
urinals? The best I see . . . are made of slate with trickling water
and a simple slate gutter at the bottom . . . in the streets of Paris."
The brothers also balked at the wood encased lavatories designed
by Root, "all the wash bowls are to be boarded up with a door
underneath, a good receptacle for dirt, mice, too. . . . This
covering up of pipes is all a mistake, they should be exposed
everywhere, if necessary painted well and handsomely." Form
follows function.

There was something else that created the skyscraper,
something behind high land prices, electric inventions, and
penny pinching Boston capitalists. Power and speed. The switch
in the nation and the city from burning trees to burning coal to
generating electricity increased the amount of power available
and the amount of power increased the pace of activities. This
was the force hammering out skyscrapers, sewer systems, transportation snarls and hoped-for solutions.

This is not the same as saying that changes always bring new
challenges, that increases in size and numbers bring new problems which force men to create new solutions. With the flows of
energy something else is going on. As power increases it creates
new structures and new speeds of movement. This in turn calls
for more power and greater speeds for the solution. Crowded
streets of horsedrawn carriages led to trains, trucks, cars—

not to paths for walking. The more power applied, the larger the problem and the less successful the solution. Each step in the ladder of growth and solution becomes more cumbersome. For example, a skyscraper, a vertical office, is more taxing per square foot than a horizontal one because everything must be lifted and the building itself grows ever more expensive and heavier with each foot of elevation in order to have strength. The solution to yet more density, the skyscraper of say triple the height, simply exacerbates the same problems.

Part of the cost for the solid structure Chicago so zealously built came in the form of bills Chicago never paid. There were the poor. While the city dreamt of monuments, the citizens packed their suitcases and endlessly moved and prowled the sprawling districts from apartment to apartment, flat to flat. Behind the prosperous facade of the downtown and the parks and the boulevards was a hurly burly of people that appalled reformers. In the city of neighborhoods, nobody seemed willing to stay put in a neighborhood. Settlement house workers led by Jane Addams sought to end this movement. Believing that the American village was the model for civic life, they attempted to foster villages in the industrial districts but were confronted by caravans instead.

Besides movement, the settlement workers found unexpected diversity. Behind the labels of Little Italy, Greek Town, and the rest, they found blocks with a dozen or more nationalities. Little Italy held twenty odd languages per block. Some Irish enclaves held more Germans than Irish. Greek Town on Blue Island was dominated by Greek stores, not Greeks. Whatever the national look of a district, it was constantly changing. The settlement workers were among the first to have difficulty finding the neighborhood in the neighborhood.

They also were among the first to realize just how the working people in the city lived. A Dr. Wood poked around the back of the Yards in the 1870s, puzzling out the district's high cholera rate. The doctor was alarmed by the flimsy shacks and packed tenements of the area. In addition, he had a problem. When the wind blew from the slaughterhouses he felt like throwing up. The locals threw up regularly themselves. The stench was over-whelming. Most of the houses had no sewer connections, many had no privies. Men, women, children just crapped wherever they happened to be. Flies were everywhere. The city had yet to conclude that sanitation was part of the cost of structure. When epidemics continued to kill the rich along with the poor, the con-cession was made, and a Sanitary District became part of the cost of doing business, like the tunnels under the Loop, like the skyscrapers.

 Human misery and the waste of human lives was as much the product of the economy as the tall towers, the railroads, the factories, the boulevards. It was a payment, a charge avoided, ignored, largely denied. The city—The City That Works—worked by pyramiding debt in the form of diminished men, women and children, terrible housing, unfit working conditions.

The initial thing to note is that Chicago at its prime, the Chicago that became the global pattern for the industrial city, never paid these bills, never operated with these costs figured into its budget. The city that said I Will, was not willing to take up every task, meet every obligation.

Later generations giddy with federal dollars and drugged by the phrase "urban renewal" would declare that something had happened there, something akin to a meteor shower, or an earth-quake or a tidal wave, which had ruined the houses. A disaster. This was not true. Many slums were built to be slums; their mean streets often sprang from architects' blueprints.

Rich people would be appalled at living conditions in the slums and would erect model tenements. In order to keep costs down, the designs would be slowly stripped to bleak essentials—communal toilets, baths, and so forth. And after this cost-cutting, few poor people would show up rich enough to live as model poor people. The lesson was simple. The city ran fine without taking care of the people who lived in the city.

As stern reality replaced all memory of the green-shuttered city in the garden, dreams began to seize the minds of those who thought about the city and about other cities. Some looked at the slums, at the filth, at the babble of tongues, the madness of the street alive with burning fires of Europe, and imagined neighborhoods, settlement houses, communities waiting, yearning to be born. They thought a dash of education, or a new ordinance, or a new alderman, or prayer would unite the masses and end the horror. Their dream was crushed by out-migration of the district's inhabitants and the constant replenishment of poor people with yet new, poorer people, the replacement of one strange tongue with another and another.

Others ignored the lives of the mass of humans and the work of the city as a whole, and said Chicago needed a plan to make sense of itself. Daniel Burnham led this movement, which culminated in 1909 in the Chicago Plan, sponsored by local merchants and capitalists. Burnham believed men should dream not small dreams but large ones which would stir men's souls. As early as 1897, he had suggested to the Merchant's Club, "You are the men who have made Chicago, who have fought her battles, who have never been content to pause and rest after deeds accomplished. . . . " Then Burnham sprang his idea: " . . . I suggest that the time has come for Chicago to make herself attractive."

The plan was parks and boulevards strung along the Lake and following the city's diagonal avenues. Large public buildings would cluster near the shore and gaze across the waters. Everything would look as if the Romans did the work and as if Parisians lived in Chicago. Come evening, or say a Sunday afternoon in Burnham's watercolors of this Chicago, herds of humans would promenade green boulevards, walking under canopies of trees to galleries, museums and theaters.

Unlike the dream of the settlements, Burnham's dream was largely feasible because it did not entail touching much of the city's life. Like beauty itself, the plan was skin deep. Where it did concern itself with inherent flows and processes in Chicago, such as in a desire to consolidate all the railroads into one yard and station, the plan got nowhere. The Chicago Plan would become a national and international model for how to think order and still do business. By wrapping the predatory nature of urban life in a new glistening skin, it showed the way for future generations of planners and city-beautiful junkies.

So you have the condition: a city exploding with energy but no social purpose, a city dedicated to funneling flows and choking on its own dedication. Three major responses result from this condition. Political graft, which looks no further than its own palm. Settlement houses, which look for salvation in attitudes and misread the ambitions and destinies of the poor. And, finally, city planning, which does not really plan the city at all but rather gift-wraps its unexamined nature and structure. All the problems humans associate with modern industrial Chicago were present at its genesis, the only change has been that the cost of the problems has made them harder to ignore. The lives of the poor, the pull of the suburban belt, the burden of antiquated structure all scream louder and louder for attention.

Clues began to appear long ago. New construction totaled $1,906,000,000 in 1926 (1972 dollars). This volume of brick and mortar and lumber and steel has never been equalled since. The search for economic stimuli has proven increasingly futile over the decades. In the 1920s, Mayor Big Bill Thompson straightened a stretch of the Chicago River and predicted a boom like the one triggered by the early canal. He was wrong. Later mayors were wrong about the cement serpents of the freeways, about the St. Lawrence Seaway, about the giant airport, about the hundreds of millions poured into projects called urban renewal. Population peaked in 1950, jobs and businesses began to dribble, then pour away. The hog butcher of the world lost the hogs, the lumber center of earth no more gorged on lumber, the stacker of wheat saw the stacks increasingly scatter across the Republic. Some heavy things, steel, for example, stayed, wedded to the cheap water transport. Many things left, their departure fueled by cheap petroleum. Any structure designed to enhance the flows on the old onion bog called for enormous sums of money in ratio to its promised return. The size of the flows of materials in the Midwest was limited because they were already developed; no new structure could promise dramatic increases. Having built a world, Chicago was left to live with its own creation. In American culture, this is considered doom.

The world had shifted from possible to actual, and the actual fenced in the possible. In 1893, Chicago hosted the World's Fair, boasting of its qualities so greatly that the city was dubbed by the New York press "the windy city." Burnham ramrodded the herd of architects that designed the celebration. Here the form-follows-function of the Chicago School was banned; here the pestering voices of men like the Brookses, demanding simplicity, were ignored. The Fair of 1893, called the White City, looked like a dream of Rome. All was white, and there were columns everywhere. Lagoons embraced the buildings. A few miles west lay the stockyards. A little north, the saws and hammers of Pilsen. The White City mirrored the possibilities of the dark city. That is what humans thought who visited the Fair. Henry Adams was bedeviled by the dynamo on exhibit in one of the halls because he realized the concentrated power of the device and sensed it was a kind of endless electric current, flowing to no particular end. Others marveled at the architecture and wished that the Court of Honor with its fountains and giant statuary and vistas could be their downtown, their neighborhood. This was not to be. The White City produced nothing but illusion. It was not stone or marble. The White City was plaster painted white.

At night, while open hearths roared in South Chicago and the cattle bellowed in the yards, while millions sweated the muggy night through on dirty crowded streets, the White City glowed. Floodlights lanced the sky. The tiny White City used three times the electricity of the dark city, Chicago.

8 Muck Bound

Andre gets ready for the hole. He pulls on his long underwear, then the pants, a flannel shirt. A sweater perhaps? No, no, he doesn't think so. But a coat for sure. He sits on the bed tugging at his boots. The bedstead is a strange thicket of leaves and roses made from iron. Andre created it. But that was another kind of work, things he did before he went down into the hole. Finally, he is ready. He is sealed from the cold, the slime, the chill of the muck. Andre gets into his car and drives to work through the warm July night.

The hole never shuts down and Andre is foreman on the grave-yard shift. On his way to the job, he thinks of better jobs. Around on Lake Shore Drive, over the river, he muses, now there's a job. They're going to put a bridge in to straighten Lake Shore Drive out at Wacker. That'll be a fine job, by God. Up in the sunshine and you can see women walk by and if you want to walk off the job for a bit, why, what's to stop you? I'd like a job like that.

The hole he works is wet and cold. The men dress heavily and keep one eye peeled for arthritis. No women ever walk by, their breasts ready to bounce out of their summer clothes. The car cuts through Grant Park where the big Labor Day bicycle races are held—just like in his native Luxembourg. Then he peels off on the Stevenson and parallels the river's South Branch. He is just south of Pilsen. Take the exit, then a left and another left and into a meadow of several acres by the River. Odd, the trees and grass and trash in the heart of Chicago. Lights, brilliant lights like a missile launch was about to take place, or a moon landing.

153

There, in the middle of the bright lights on the July night in Chicago, the hole.

> Chicago is peculiarly fortunate in having a *system* of sewers. In most cities, it has been the practice to construct individual sewers from time to time, according to the want of the particular street or district to be drained, and without any general plan for the drainage of the entire city. In after years, as it became necessary to use them as general sewers, they have often been found inadequate as to capacity, or useless from being at unsuitable grades or elevation. In Chicago each sewer is a link in the system, and designed to fulfill its work as part of the whole. The change or relaying of a permanent sewer has never yet been necessary.
> —Eighth Annual Report of the
> Board of Public Works, 1869

Trailers are scattered about the gravel lot, the river runs silent in the darkness. The units serve as office, lockroom, power-house. The place has the feel of a construction site, all raw and temporary. In a trailer stuffed with electric generators, pin-ups gleaned from Larry Flynt's *Hustler* paper the walls.

Andre parks, walks to the office, puts on his hard hat and readies himself to run the next shift. Only about a dozen men work the shift with him. One man runs the giant crane which towers over the lot like a praying mantis. The crane lowers the other men two hundred fifty feet into the hole.

The men have gathered here to fix Chicago's eighth wonder of the world, its sanitary system. Originally, the plan had been simple. The flow of the Chicago River was reversed so that it did not empty into the Lake. The city took its drinking water from the Lake. Treated sewage was then dumped into the reversed river and it became in effect an oxidizing ditch. This solution often failed because the city used a single sewer system for both sewage and storm waters. About every three or four days on the average a storm overwhelmed the capacity of the sewers, and sewage backed up into basements or poured out into the streets or overflowed into the River or rose to such heights that crap streamed into the Lake and the drinking water. The hole was part of the strategy to stop this violation of the water supply.

A series of deep tunnels would be dug paralleling the Chicago River's branches. When the rains came and the sewers were overwhelmed, these deep tunnels would be filled with sewage. When the storm passed and the system returned to its normal levels, these deep tunnels would be pumped empty and the sewage returned to the system for treatment. Eventually, so the plan figured it, all fifty-three communities in the Chicago area would be hooked up to the deep tunnels. They would be deep in earth, deep in the heart of the aquifer from which the suburban communities were forced by court order to pump their drinking water from wells. Everyone hoped that the tunnels would not leak.

For those who argue against the size of cities, that they are too big to manage, here was a big answer. For those who despair of dealing with the complicated problems of urban life, here was a simple cure. For those who said Chicago was the problem, here was an instance where Chicago claimed a solution.

For where else are men like Andre leaving home on a July evening dressed for winter in order to dig tunnels two hundred fifty feet under the earth to be filled with shit and piss?

> In 1851, when the population was about 35,000 . . . the present works were commenced. . . . The Chief Engineer, Mr. Wm. J. McAlpine said:
> "It is very questionable whether the small quantity of water which is discharged from the river would affect the quality of the water in the lake at a point one and half miles south. . . ."

In 1860, one of the Water Commissioners, Mr. Edward Hamilton, proposed to sink a wrought iron pipe, 5 feet in diameter, one mile out in the lake to obtain a supply of water beyond the effect of the river. . . .

. . . It was thought best to defer the whole subject until further examination and analysis could be made, in the hope that much of the complaint against the water supply might prove imaginary.

What however was at first apparent only to the most sensitive organizations, soon grew evident to all, and in the course of two or three years more, the water supply became occasionally very offensive to both the taste and smell. A remedy for this state of things could no longer be neglected.

—Eighth Annual Report of the Board
of Public Works, 1869

To descend, Andre climbs into a bucket with a wire cage, signals the crane operator, and begins to drop. There are many layers of Chicago to penetrate before the deep tunnel can be reached.

very soft blue clay
soft blue clay
medium blue clay
stiff blue clay
hard blue clay
miscellaneous fill
stiff yellow clay
very stiff yellow clay
hard yellow clay
sand
yellow sand
gray sand
sand and boulders

Down through the sediment of time until the dolomite, a gray rock and the home of the tunnel. Look up as the bucket slowly sinks and the image is a well, those fabled wells of the plains, where a man at the bottom could see stars at noon. The night is overcast. The men talk as they sink to their shift. Then the bottom, an exit, a signal and the bucket ascends, leaving the crew below. The walls are gray, damp and electric lit. The tunnel, thirty-two feet in diameter, goes off to the southwest. A railroad runs down the center to haul away the rock. There is hope it can be peddled for concrete. Here and there on the floor is litter— a pop can, an old pack of Lucky Strikes. Human history has already begun in the tunnel.

Many do not know the tunnels are being dug; until the past year, hardly anyone was aware of the project. They came into being to meet federal water standards, to alleviate pollution of homes, of the River, of the Lake. Who is going to argue about a sewer project? Or care?

The deep tunnels are models for all the cities in the United States that must, and supposedly will, meet water quality standards, that must and will remedy the legacy of filth left by the industrial boom of the nineteenth century. There is but one problem with the model. Or, more accurately, one *big* problem. It is said to be the most expensive public works project ever attempted, and the cost keeps rising. As Andre alights on the wet floor of his tunnel, it is apparent that tubes for waste in Chicago will cost eight to twelve billion dollars. Billion.

Work has been going on for awhile; there is a walk to the mine face. One learns to step tie to tie along the electric railroad; this keeps the feet clear of the muck. The air is neither stale nor fresh; lungs breathe oxygen circulated down the shaft by machines, air like in a 747 or a department store elevator, neither stale nor fresh. Andre lights a cigarette and strides forward to the task.

The tunnel walls are identical every foot of the way, almost smooth in finish. The mole did it. Everything in the tunnel is the mole. The diameter? The mole's diameter. Speed? The mole's speed. Direction? Forward. Moles don't go back.

Andre was not trained up to the mole. He is an ironworker helping to gouge a giant cesspool. In Luxembourg, when he did his stint in the army, he was the armorer responsible for the sabres, rifles and other weapons of war. He learned as an apprentice to fashion iron into any form. In his twenties, he came to Chicago. There was plenty of work designing fancy gates and window grilles for millionaires in the suburbs. But the work did not pay. Then everything was interrupted by Vietnam, and he was gone to Canada to duck the draft.

Now he was back, and back in the hole. He still has his touch. His wife is opening a gourmet cook shop full of odd pots and pans. One night when work is slack in the hole, Andre takes a sheet of iron, sketches on a drawing of a fat Dutch chef holding a cleaver in one hand and a dead goose in the other. Liberates it from the metal with a cutting torch. A sign for the shop.

But lately it has been the mole.

It came down the hole piece by piece, a model kit like those for twelve-year-olds. Andre put the model together, week after week. What finally emerged was a multimillion-dollar machine that looks a block long and, when all is said and done, replaces men with picks and shovels. Andre is the mole's keeper and when the mole feels ill, he is called for. He probes the innards, checks the giant bearings, tests the blood pressure of the lubricating system, adjusts the immense power train, and aligns the laser beam eye. He has a feeling for the beast. Andre says the mole is a hell of a lot of machine for only a couple of million dollars. A special machine. In the whole earth, this is the right place for this mole. Everything here was built to its scale, and it was built to the scale of everything here.

This is home, and Andre, warm in his long underwear on the July night, is the mole's guardian.

> The principal mining shaft was under the inspection of Mr. Dewer, an experienced miner. His chief duties were to keep the excavation within proper lines and to watch for the approach of bad ground. . . . This shift consisted of four miners and four pushers. . . .
>
> The general custom was for two miners to work together for ten or fifteen minutes at a time with more than common vigor and then rest. The pushers loaded the excavated earth into the cars, brought as near the face as possible on a moveable truck. . . .
>
> —Eighth Annual Report of the
> Board of Public Works, 1869

The walk along the tracks ends. The pushers of 1869 have become an entire subterranean railroad to haul the waste expelled by the mole. The end of the tunnel looks like it is plugged by a ramshackle shed. This is the mole. No need for a sleek aerodynamic form down here. It is difficult to believe this thing can move and devour rock. From the rear the mole is a maze of pipes, wires, catwalks, doors, stairways. A closer look finds the stubby legs on which the mole crawls forward ten, twenty, maybe thirty feet per day. Men scamper around the machine, oiling and checking its belts and bearings. One man drives the mole sitting in a simple cabin with a few controls and a laser gun.

> For the alignment of the tunnel an astronomical transit of four inch aperture, by Pike of New York, was mounted on a tower built for this purpose, 166 feet westward of the land shaft. . . . To aid in placing the lake shaft beyond all doubt in the line of the tunnel, a 6-inch tube was sunk 280 feet eastward of the land shaft. . . .
>
> —Eighth Annual Report of the
> Board of Public Works, 1869

The mole was guided by the laser, the magic fire of the twentieth century. Up in front of the driver was the cutting face, a disc with fangs that swirled and ate a wall thirty-two feet in diameter.

That was it, a small crew of a dozen working with a multimillion dollar mole to follow a laser into a stratum of dolomite rock. Most of the men scrambling around the mole oiling and tightening were laborers making twenty to thirty thousand a year. A few men to run the railroad, one man to drive the mole, and Andre to solve problems as they arose and to see to the beast's care and feeding. These operations would dig a tunnel to store waste two hundred fifty feet below the surface. All adding up to a hole costing hundreds of millions of dollars and part of a network of holes costing billions.

That is assuming everything went all right. Sometimes the mole dug erratically. It almost never made it through an eight-hour shift without breaking down. Sometimes it dug too well and spewed rock and dust behind it at a rate that overwhelmed the little railroad and thus slowly buried itself in the tunnel it was digging. When this happened Andre had a phrase for it.

The mole was muck bound.

> Very soon the miners learned to detect the proximity of
> cavities containing this gas from the sound produced by
> striking over them with their picks. When a cavity was thus
> detected, it was bored into with a small auger, the gas ig-
> nited as soon as it began to escape. . . . The explosions that
> did occur were slight in character, but left a body of flame in
> the upper part of the tunnel. At such times the miners fell
> with their faces to the ground, and thus escaped without any
> greater injury than singed beards and eyelashes and blis-
> tered faces, except in the first severe case when a miner was
> severely burnt. At this time gas kept the miners out of the
> tunnel three days.
>
> —Eighth Annual Report of the
> Board of Public Works, 1869

Sometimes the mole broke. Two hundred fifty feet down in the earth beneath the city that was burying itself in its own wastes, the mole stopped moving and lay idle. Wedged into the tunnel with a laser eye, the beast wouldn't move. The mole that had been lowered into the hole piece by piece, that Andre had slowly and patiently assembled, the mole that was exactly the size of the tunnel it dug, was broken. No driver could throw it into reverse and pull off under an inviting shady oak tree for repairs. No wrecker could come and seize the mole's bumper and haul it off to the garage. The mole was the tool that was going to save Chicago with a twelve billion dollar solution, and now the mole was stuck in the solution. It must be treated on the spot.

For several weeks, the men had been tearing it apart, all three shifts a day, reaching slowly with wrench and hammer into its mechanical heart and seeking the hurt that stalled it. Boards were loosely tossed here and there for more catwalks. Andre and the men scampered over the wobbly pieces of lumber to look in here, to inspect something there. They pored over blueprints for clues. The fine powder that filled the air when the mole was digging was gone and the tunnel was relatively still and clean.

It would be weeks before the mole would start up again. And after that, the time would come when the mole would break again. And again. Andre was confident that this job was good for years. It had that kind of scale.

In Chicago in the 1980s, it took the largest public works project in history to alleviate, not to end but to alleviate, sewage backups and overflows, to return the Chicago River from a state of vileness to one of filth. It took twelve billion dollars, and the mole. And the mole broke.

Andre had to go up again, check the blueprints, and look for clues. He was a patient man. He liked the mole, a helluva lot of machine for only a couple of million. He was working on some-

thing bigger than anything else ever attempted. A hole in the
ground, costing billions that few would ever see, and that would
be filled with waste. Andre did not talk diseconomies of scale, or
entropy and the deep tunnels being the same, or wonder if the city
could afford the cost of its increasingly enormous remedies.
   Enough of that.
   Andre was just grateful for the mole.
   What a machine!
   A laser eye, a thirty-two foot cutting face.
   A helluva lot of machine for a couple of million dollars.

   The original estimate of the probable cost of the work was
   $307,552. The actual cost . . . was $457,844.95 . . . . Connected with the construction of a work of this kind, there
   was necessarily very much of interest that cannot here be
   repeated. The journals of the day published many articles
   relative to the tunnel, some purely descriptive, some
   speaking favorably of the enterprise, and many unfavor-
   ably. Since completion, visitors to the city who reside hundreds, and in some cases thousands of miles away,
   frequently say, "we watched the progress of your work with
   great interest."
                              —The Eighth Annual Report of the Board
                                    of Public Works, Chicago, 1869

very soft blue clay
soft blue clay
medium blue clay
stiff blue clay
very stiff blue clay
hard blue clay.

9 Benny Goodman Lived Here

Diane's been looking for a neighborhood. Today, the problem is called condominium. Her apartment is being converted to the joys of home ownership. If you have twenty or thirty or forty grand stuffed under the mattress, this is swell. If not, you move. Diane has moved three times because her apartments have been converted to condos. That's the kind of city Chicago is, a city that makes you move. Diane accepts that fact. It makes her angry but she accepts it.

Diane does not have broad shoulders. She has slender shoulders and high cheekbones. Her pumps are maroon, a thin gold chain around her ankle. She works downtown in an office now. She used to work on the West Side. In Lawndale. She was a black woman working in a black organization trying to create a black community in a place called Lawndale. She did not accept things so easily in those days. Nobody had heard of condos then. Beginning in the 60's people like Diane were trying to create something thought to be traditional in Lawndale. They were putting together a neighborhood.

In the city famous for neighborhoods, Lawndale was a famous neighborhood. Real estate developers in the 1870s coined the name. Just about the time they had the streets and parks laid out the Great Fire leveled much of the city and provided an eager market. The area was bordered eventually by two railroads, a Western Electric plant and the world headquarters of Sears, Roebuck and Company. In the early to mid twentieth century Lawndale had been solidly Jewish; now Lawndale contained 176,000 people and was 92.6% black.

People in Lawndale did not know they lived in Lawndale. When asked, they'd say they lived on the West Side and let it go at that. In the 1960s Martin Luther King, Jr. came to Lawndale and moved into a flat to draw attention to the bad housing and high rents. When neighborhood organizers visited local elementary schools a few years later, the kids did not know that King had ever been in Lawndale. For that matter they did not know they lived in Lawndale. Whites knew who lived in Lawndale; they read it in the newspapers.

In 1965, 1966, and 1968 riots led to the sacking of businesses along Pulaski Avenue and Roosevelt Road. In 1970, the Model Cities program did a survey of housing in Lawndale and found that in a sixty day period nearly 100 buildings were abandoned by landlords who had squeezed the bricks dry of rents. This was the Lawndale that existed in the crime statistics, housing statistics and newspaper headlines but not in the minds of the people who lived there. Diane and others set out to change this.

They wanted Lawndale to fit the traditional idea of a neighborhood. The district would be a stable place where people worked, bought homes, married and buried. Everybody said this was what neighborhoods were all about. Everywhere they looked in Lawndale they saw evidence of this fact. Forty nine synagogues stood abandoned on the boulevards. Scattered about the block were former old folks homes, religious schools, libraries, hospitals, clubs, kosher markets, shopping strips, parks, playgrounds.

The Jews had really put Lawndale on the map. They had had political clout. Jake Arvey had walked these streets and by the late forties he was hailed as a king-maker, a man who made presidents. Behind Arvey were the Rosenbergs, Moe and Ike, who represented a consortium of criminals. They delivered the votes of the Twenty-Fourth Ward, of which Lawndale was a piece, and for their trouble were left alone in the Twenty-Fourth Ward. This was a neighborhood. Everybody agreed on that. Diane and others looked at the ruins of Lawndale in the sixties and said, "This is where the power was."

They set out to restore the past. The blacks had seen enough "changing neighborhoods." They had seen their movement into an area as the official explanation for tumult and decay. Many whites felt blacks had ruined the city. In Lawndale they had taken note of the charge, and sought to escape the world of changing neighborhoods for the promised land of the Neighborhood.

But this proved a difficult task because they sought something that had not existed. The blacks sought to put down roots on rootless ground.

First had come the Dutch, the Irish and the Germans, driven west by the destruction of the 1871 Fire and drawn by the relocation of McCormick's reaper works on nearby Western Avenue. Following this initial spurt, the area's expansion stalled until after the turn of the century. Then the elevated penetrated the district on its way to Cicero, and Western Electric and Sears moved in to feed off the railways. These brought workers.

After the 1905 revolution in Russia, the Czar's subjects began killing Jews again and this sent new masses of Jews in flight to America and to Chicago, and in Chicago, to Maxwell Street on the Near West Side. Jews settled along the street since the eighties and nineties greeted their co-religionists and then fled further west to Lawndale. The Dutch, Irish, and Germans refused to rent and tried to hold the line. The Jews, desperate to escape their old neighborhood of Maxwell Street, met this resistance by buying whole buildings, vacant lots, even entire blocks. By 1915, Lawndale was Jewish. The area's population in 1910 had been 46,000, and by 1920, it was 93,750.

The gentiles were leaving or gone. There goes the neighborhood.

Before the Jews took Lawndale, the basic type of building had been the two-flat, but from 1915 on the contractors threw up large apartment buildings, usually with twenty units or more. This boom continued until the Great Crash of 1929. Lawndale's borders stayed the same, its population rose to 112,000 (75,000 Jewish) in 1930. The result was remarkable density of settlement. While the tough Chicago of the novels of Nelson Algren and James Farrell had 25,000 humans per packed mile, Lawndale held 51,000. The only place that could match this density was Grand Boulevard in the Black Belt. Lawndale—kosher Calcutta.

> For more than three seasons, Carl Ballantine played Lester
> Grubber on the TV series, 'McHale's Navy . . . . ' Sure, I'm
> from the West Side,' he says, rolling his blue eyes and
> waggling his cigar like Jack E. Leonard from Division St.
> 'My barber got me interested in magic. He'd come to the
> house, give me a half-buck haircut, and pull herrings and
> chickens out of his sleeve. Who could afford a rabbit?'
> —Chicago *Daily News*

This mass of humanity became the center of the city's Jewish institutions. By 1930, Lawndale had forty synagogues, many staffed by graduates of the Hebrew Theological College, which had moved to the area in 1922. Herzl Junior College began its program in 1935; the Jewish People's Institute, dedicated to adult education, came in 1927. For laboring Jews, there was Workman's Circle, which in turn sponsored the Lyceum Players, a Yiddish theater. For homeless children, the Mark Nathan Orphanage; for the aged, Orthodox Jewish Home for the Aged. For the sick, the Jewish People's Convalescent Home, Mount Sinai Hospital, Rest Haven Rehabilitation Hospital. Send a boy to camp? The Young Men's Jewish Council.

These were the backbone of what would be remembered as the Jewish community on the West Side. Lawndale was the monument to those Jews who broke out of the ghetto of Maxwell Street and sought to forge a life that was both Jewish and part of the twentieth century. This was their improvement on the homeland, just as a later Lawndale would be for many blacks a new version of the South.

> At the 24th Ward headquarters, 3604 W. Roosevelt, in an imposing old brick building that looks as though it once might have been a bank, Horwitz was talking about the congressional race. . . .
> Horwitz told how, when the Jews ran the ward, funerals were paid for, free matzohs were handed out at high holiday times, food baskets suddenly appeared for needy families and help in getting jobs done was provided.
> —Chicago *Sun Times,*
> November 4, 1970

This is the Lawndale that betwitches the present. Strong, stable, nourished with free matzohs. The Douglas branch of the Chicago Public Library shelved 3500 volumes in Yiddish. One synagogue of the many on the boulevard seated 3500 people. This was a community built on a large scale and with an intention to last. Surely. Chicago politicians had to kowtow to this Lawndale. This memory of Lawndale has force because events froze it in time for fifteen years. Between the Crash of 1929 and the end of World War II, unemployment and lack of new housing combined to give many neighborhoods in Chicago and elsewhere a false sense of security against change. From this stagnation arose a dreamland, a place where Studs Lonigan was always courting Lucy on a park bench. Thanks to mass unemployment, international warfare and a collapsed housing industry, the idea of neighborhood as a stable place has come down the years as wisdom beyond debate. Every variance from this is an unex-

pected deviation from the norm. This has left us cities of constant
motion where the motion is seen as a fall from a state of grace.
Always there was a time when people pulled together, knew one
another, took an interest in where they lived and stayed put. Even
in Lawndale. Remember?

It has been years since Ben Bentley scuffled his way out of
the third floor tenement apartment just off Roosevelt Road
and into his present role as a hustling promoter. But on
Tuesday afternoon, Bentley was riding through the old
West Side neighborhood again on a sentimental journey.
As he rode he kept studying the black kids who were playing
in the streams of water from the open hydrants.

'Who says they shouldn't play in the water?' Bentley said
as the car pulled up to Francisco Street. 'What the hell else
can they do? There's no place else for them to go.'

Suddenly Bentley realized where he was. 'Stop the car,'
he said. 'Look down the street. Right here on Francisco.
This is where Benny Goodman used to live. Right there in
that third house on the left hand side.'

'My God, when I think of it. What great people came out
of this neighborhood.'

—Chicago *Sun Times,* June 30, 1971

Why did the Jews leave? The usual answer in Chicago for such
matters is blacks. Pushing in, block busting. There goes the
neighborhood. The usual answer is often wrong. To begin with,
the Jews packed into the district lacked any deep economic ties to
the district. Surrounded by factories, they tended to work elsewhere. Lawndale did not have one of the most essential attributes
of the dream neighborhood of memory—it did not combine residence and work. Also, Lawndale was founded as a way station,
not a destination. It was a place where ghetto Jews shook the
ghetto from their lives and minds before they moved on. In the
end, it was not far enough away from the ghetto to be an end to
flight. Still, it is difficult to confront forty synagogues, various

hospitals and schools and sense that this place is a brief resting point. The brick and mortar insist that this is for keeps. This is the neighborhood.

> 'What will become of our children?' said Rabbi Saul
> Silber . . . 'Do we want them to grow up pinochle players
> and poker sharks, or do we want them to grow up men and
> women who have an understanding of the problems of life,
> who know the history of their ancestors, who are proud
> Jews and who will be a credit to us? Our children are
> running away from us because we have nothing to hold
> them with. . . .'
>   Well spoken, Rabbi Silber. It is unfortunate that the
> Jewish population has the moving spirit and neighborhoods
> change practically overnight. First it was Douglas and
> Independence Boulevards, then the North Shore District,
> then Rogers Park; now it is Wilmette, Winnetka, Glencoe,
> etc. These newly rich want to be 'swell' and to be 'swell' is to
> run away from Jews and Judaism—that's the modern
> curse.
>   —Chicago *Chronicle,* January 16, 1925.

Between 1930 and 1940, the population of Lawndale declined by 10,000. The old stayed, but the young left. Almost everyone who got out was under 45; the proportion of people over sixty-five increased 50%. Between 1940 and 1950, the change continued. Besides becoming a reservoir of the old, Lawndale increasingly became the home of lower income people, as residents who made a buck quickly moved the money to a better neighborhood. Lawndale filled with new immigrants. Of the seventy-five districts in the city, Lawndale had the highest proportion of foreign-born in 1930, 1940, and 1950. At the time of the Crash, 45% of the area's population was immigrant, mainly from Russia and Poland.

Still, by statistics and charts the district held as a Jewish
stronghold; the population was 67% Jewish in 1930 and 64%
Jewish in 1946. Then came the end of World War II and the end
of restraints on new construction.

In 1950, Lawndale was 42% Jewish. The population of
139,700 held 13,300 blacks, 9.5% of the total. By 1960, 190,450
humans were crammed into Lawndale—149,950 of them black.
Seven years later the area was 90% black, and Lawndale had
switched from being the escape from the ghetto to the new
ghetto. Insitutional change in the area almost kept pace with the
population shift. Herzl Junior College was made an elementary
school in 1953. The Jewish People's Institute and the Hebrew
Theological College were peddled to the city as new public
schools. In 1955, the Labor Lyceum of Workman's Circle was
sold to a black church. The collection of Judaica in the public
library was shifted to a North Side branch.

Within the simple fact that blacks replaced Jews on the census
tracts lay the elements of a myth: the loss of Lawndale. The district that had a density surpassed only by a strip in the black belt,
the place that was the home of such rowdy bands of boys as the
Deuces Wild, Jovens, Diamond Eagles, Redskins, and Sionilli,
the place so stuffed with tenements that the only lawns were in
the public parks, became the beloved homeland in memory. As
Jews fled into a gleeful diaspora to the suburbs and northern
sections of the city, the Lawndale left behind became a cherished
ideal of community.

The car pulled into a gas station and Ben leaped out to
supervise the work of the attendant.
'You know,' Ben said to the attendant, 'I grew up in this
neighborhood.'
The attendant smiled in disbelief.
'Yeah,' said Ben, 'I lived just a couple of blocks away. I

never had enough money to live on Douglas.

'Jake Arvey lived on this block. I remember the first time I saw Mayor Edward J. Kelly he was pulling up to Arvey's house on a Sunday afternoon.

'That's the kind of thing that used to happen here. . . . '

Bentley thought for a minute realizing perhaps that it's been at least 30 years since he moved away from Roosevelt Road.

Then he said, 'Don't get me wrong. I was never a rich kid. I didn't even have a real bed to sleep on until my older sister got married and I was able to move off the couch.'

Bentley stopped the car.

'Look at all those boarded up windows,' he said. 'I can't take it anymore. Let's go back downtown.'

—Chicago *Sun Times,* June 30, 1971

Jewish Lawndale joined the pantheon of Chicago neighborhoods in the city of neighborhoods. The place once had a smart commercial district, institutions of higher learning, hospitals, lectures, library, synagogues. Come a summer evening people would be sitting out on the stoops talking with one another, and did they vote, boy, the Twenty-Fourth Ward is a legend, they elected Presidents, had their own man, Jake Arvey. A great place, Lawndale.

Black people inherited this Lawndale. To be sure, they also got the Lawndale that in the 1950 census featured numerous buildings without private baths—seventeen blocks in the district having over 50% of the buildings innocent of working private baths or any flush toilets at all. They got an area whose housing stock predated the Great Depression and which for at least twenty years had been subjected to overcrowding and deterioration. They got a place that even with its proximity to Jewish institutions was not worth living in for most Jews. And they got the memory of the great Lawndale, the economically sound

Lawndale, the spiffy, squeaky clean Lawndale, the powerful
Lawndale to haunt them as they struggled in a real ghetto and
tried to make do in a real slum. Blacks got the failures of the past
and were told they got the real goods.⟩

In a city characterized by free movement, they were the only
ones forced to stay put. In a city that was in fact uninterested in
neighborhoods, they sought to construct one from worn out
tenements that never could be the basis of community. In a city
united only by its antipathy to blacks, they attempted to follow a
legendary model of Jewish progress and Irish political smarts.
Here in Lawndale, Diane and many others following in the wake
of Martin Luther King's crusade to desegregate Chicago, put
their shoulders to the wheel to push onward to the community.
Like the Mexicans in Pilsen and the South Side blacks scrambling
into square miles abandoned by the white flight to the suburbs,
they reached for a piece of the kingdom that had brought them to
the city by the lake. As one black woman explained her struggle
to buy a house in Lawndale, "In my father's house there are
many mansions and I'm going to get me some of them, too!"

There goes the neighborhood.

What came after the legend of the past with its cosy neighborhoods of ethnic purity was the rhetoric and folklore of the
present. Beneath the buzz of racism, sexism, and revolution,
people bought homes in Lawndale and supported churches in
Lawndale and struggled up the job ladders to higher skills and
wages. They participated in a national movement that brought
civil rights for blacks out of the law books and attic of the Consti-
tution and into the daily life of the nation. And three times in the
sixties, 1965, 1966, and 1968, the people of Lawndale tried to tear
the place they lived down to the boggy soil it was built on.

⟨The forces which had built Chicago left Lawndale largely
alone. The freeways and the railroads went by the district but

brought little in and took little out. The huge International Harvester plant on Western Avenue lay idle and then was demolished. The reapers went off and left Chicago to its own harvest. Sears trekked downtown and climbed a tower 110 stories high, its Lawndale facility increasingly becoming the back room. By the 1970s, Lawndale's largest asset was its emptiness. In a city choking on intractable structure, this neighborhood hosted acre after acre of vacant land—95 acres at the Harvester site alone. Abandoned buildings promised even more. In Lawndale, according to one local group, "the center commercial core . . . around Roosevelt Road has never recovered from the destruction during the nineteen sixty riots and it looks horrifyingly similar to the bombed out cities of Europe at the close of World War II." What houses stood were either prey to landlords of little means who could barely afford the buildings and had no funds for repairs or owned by rich men who lived in blind trusts and who refrained from spending profits on restorations. Many structures too close to the edge of profit and loss were abandoned.

Such conditions invited rescue. One scheme floated by a private developer would have used Model Cities funds to bulldoze 190 acres then housing poor black people. The bare earth would have received 12,500 units pegged at middle and upper middle class paychecks, plus a forty-five acre golf course.

Like Pilsen, dilapidated Lawndale seems to raise an urban planner's blood to a fever pitch. Local people reacted by putting forth their own plans and getting their own Model Cities backing and wound up pushing for a new high school, a shopping center, an old folks' home and buying the vacant Harvester land for the site of an industrial park. The Lawndale of memory with busy stores, jobs and local institutions was going to be restored with one fell swoop of the federal checkbook.

It was here that Diane and many others put their shoulders to the wheel. In a Chicago of dwindling flows where capital and work fled to the suburbs and to the deep South and the West, a landing pad was offered for industry that for decades had been looking for the exit sign. Around this industrial heart, the plan placed all the elements felt essential to community—health, education, housing, shopping. Lawndale was to be fixed up "as a community for the people who now live there. . . . " All this has been slow, very slow in coming. Partly because the Democratic organization is not keen on the plan. Partly because downtown businessmen are doubtful at times and hostile at times. Partly because federal agencies move slowly and wobble in their intentions. But mainly, land is vacant in Lawndale because people and industry would rather be elsewhere. The forces that broke the district are unlikely to restore it except in a token fashion.

Lawndale continues as an industrial slum, without the industry. The place invites theories that explain the plagues of the modern city. Some say it is all race, that the blacks have done in the neighborhood. Some say it is racism, that hatred of blacks has done in the neighborhood. Then there are various formulas of venture capital, a million here and a million there, better schools, day care centers, improved garbage pickup, let's fix up the flats and tenements, and no lead paint. Or it's the middle class that's lacking, and always it is seen as easier to import these creatures than to grow them afresh from the bulldozed land. Urban renewal, new town in town, gentrification, industry, slum clearance. A model city.

None of it works and all of it works. Things get better but never get to that destination, that place of memory where Lawndale is a community full of paychecks and stores and local institutions and clout. Where the old ward organization plied voters with free matzohs, the current one holds Christmas parties for the kids, banquets for the aged, and once a year lines up the buses so that 10,000 local children get hauled off for an annual Lawndale picnic. Always there remains this gap between the plan and the street. Finally, some say it takes time to climb the golden ladder to the middle class, a generation or two or three to struggle through the factory machines and emerge wearing a white collar.

Diane keeps moving. She has had enough of time. She has had enough of community building, of neighborhood salvation. She is downtown looking out a window on LaSalle Street, where the power is, watching men across the way hang twenty floors above the street, washing windows. She has that bitterness that Chicago gives for time served. This is the most racist city in the North, says, this place never lets up. Then there are the condos stalking renters day and night. She lashes out, she is fed up and still hungry. She is stuck like the muck bound mole, only Diane is mired in thoughts. You'd think that work, and plans for industrial development and shopping centers and banks and old folks' homes and a new high school and everything, would make it happen. You'd think the paychecks would come just like they were said to in the past. She remembers the slogan, TODAY'S LAWNDALE: BLACK COLONY—TOMORROW'S LAWNDALE: NEW CITY. Enough of slogans.

They say it is a city of neighborhoods, but all she knows is moving. Why can't it be like the old days, you know? Why can't we have the jobs? And why can't we stay put and build a community?

Benny Goodman, you know, used to live in Lawndale.

178

10 Florence

Florence Scala won't move. When all the statistics and studies said that the second generation fled all the Little Italies and all the little this and thats, she stayed put. When in the 1960s the Mayor and the city fathers, in a surprise move, bulldozed most of her neighborhood for the new Chicago campus of the University of Illinois, she stayed put. When they tore down the Hull House complex that gave her youth most of its bright spots, she stayed put. When her campaign against the local alderman in 1964 drew a mixture of scorn from the old neighbors, harassing telephone calls, and outright threats of physical harm, she stayed put. She's in her fifties now, she's well-known and some people consider her a kind of saint, she's in one of Studs Terkel's books, and she still stays put.

She wonders why.

She wonders why she has stayed put, she wonders why she is still in this neighborhood she has fought to save, and she wonders what saving it means. She lives on the West Side, backed up against Lawndale, just a bit north and west of Pilsen. She has thought about the city a lot.

> I was born in Chicago, and I've always loved the city. I'm not sure anymore. I love it and I hate it everyday. What I hate is that so much of it is ugly, you see? And you really can't do very much about it. I hate the fact that so much of it is inhuman in the way we don't pay attention to each other. And we can do very little about making it human ourselves.
>
> —Florence Scala in Studs Terkel,
> *Division Street America*

179

The house was the back of the shop. Her father was a tailor, her mother helped with the pressing. They were the poor of the textbooks, but it didn't bother her much—until she was about fourteen. Then, girlfriends started to come over, and she'd go to their houses, and then she knew. In the winter, they'd all sit around warming their feet on the stove. They had enough to eat. Were the summers bad? Funny, I don't remember, you know?

Sure, they had gangsters and all that stuff. Once there was a dead man in the alley. But none of that was really important since the gangsters just killed each other. She'd go downtown on dates, and it was so bright on State Street with all the lights in the night. Then she'd come to Taylor Street on the near West Side and it would be dark, so dark. Cinderella at midnight. I hate this neighborhood. I hate the neighborhood. She can still feel it.

> Some, having a more practical vision of their potential, spent their money and their energies improving their properties, planting grass and trees on postage size lots— trying to create a space that was their own . . .
> The neighborly relationships that have spanned generations, the ability to live near black people for so long without tragic consequences—even though inter-relationships with blacks are minimal, the way some of us have survived what the city has done to us—what the commercial city and its power have done to us—that counts for something.
> —Florence Scala, letter, 1979

Her father first went to Philadelphia since that's where people from his village went. But he didn't like it, he wanted to go further west, I don't know why, he just wanted to move into the country, you know? He wanted to see two things in the United States: Niagara Falls and the Grand Canyon. The first time he went alone, then the next year he took my brothers. The next year he took me and my sisters. But the first year he just went alone, kind of wanted to scout it out, you know. We'd leave like on Friday and get back Sunday night. We took our own food and we didn't have a sleeper, you know, we just sat there the whole time in the seat.

He never made it to the Grand Canyon, got too old. My father lived to be ninety-eight and when he died, he had $19,000 in the bank. All the money, the mortgage was paid off too, all this had happened during World War II mainly. The building three stories, free and clear. I said to my brother, this is not enough. For ninety-eight years of life? He never went back to Italy. He didn't want to. He'd say, "This is my country, America."

I first got to see the country, trees, you know, rural, through the Hull House camp. You know, for the first time I'm starting to have second thoughts about Jane Addams. I've been reading her and I've noticed how she turned from the neighborhood to global and national issues, to causes, you know, peace and things.

Why'd she quit so soon?

How'd she know it was hopeless?

When one of the teachers suggested that our mother send us to Hull House, life began to open up. . . . The influence of Hull House saved the neighborhood. It never really purified it, you know what I mean? I don't think Hull House intended to do that. But it gave us . . . well, for the first time my mother left that darn old shop to attend Mother's Club once a week. She was very shy, I remember. Hull House gave you a little insight into another world. There was something else to life besides sewing and pressing.

—Florence Scala in Studs Terkel,
Division Street America

In some ways, the end of Hull House was the beginning of Florence Scala. She saw it demolished for the new state university and saw the board of Hull House, people of wealth and power, do nothing. Nothing to save Hull House, nothing to save the neighborhood from the bulldozers. She'd trusted them. She learned.

Johnny D'Arco told my brother, he said Taylor Street might be a site, and that we should get organized and get people out if they wanted to stop it. He's the alderman, he ought to know. But then Daley said, don't worry, it's just one of half a dozen sites and we're not looking that seriously at it. So nobody did anything.

When I tried to organize to stop the university, only ten, maybe fifteen families outside the condemned area would help. There was fear, real fear. John didn't want to mix in. Sympathetic, but . . . .Everybody has jobs with the city. There was fear, you know?

So I ran for alderman and I got to learn a lot of things. There were phone calls, all the time. Every night fire trucks came to the house, somebody calling in false alarms. You go to vote and there was this black woman there at the polls with the fierce police dog snarling. They'd do things like that, the organization. So I ran against Daley and I ran against the syndicate and I got one-third of the votes and everybody said great, look how many votes you got and I said, are you crazy? What about the other two-thirds?

> It doesn't count for enough—I know . . . . Most of us who are still here have survived as *victims*. . . .
>   Are we only spectators to the bigger event—after all— is Chicago life and government just a festival where we can no longer párticipate except as audience?
>   —Florence Scala, letter, 1979

Last year, you know, Jane Byrne came down to Holy Family when she was trying to get the mayor's nomination and she got up and talked and there was only a dozen or so of us there, and she started talking about JFK and RFK. And I asked her, I said, you know, these people are dead so why are you talking about them? Why don't you tell us what you will do? And she didn't answer, you know. She has this habit if she doesn't like a question of just nodding her head and then going on like you didn't exist or something. So I asked her again and I said you know I'm not trying to be negative you know but what do these dead people have to do with what you're going to do in Chicago, I mean they're gone, what are you going to do? And she didn't answer me.

She came down here to get the neighborhood votes, you know, and there was this dead dog in the street, and she was horrified, like she'd never seen such a thing, and she said this has to be changed, this must be fixed, stopped, you know? She doesn't know how people live in this city. She was shook up.

I want a place in the country. I want trees and grass. My mother would tell me of walking to work, this was back in the old country, walking to work in fields and just reaching up and picking fruit from the trees.

I'd ask her, did you really do that? Did you really just reach up and pick fruit off the trees?

Yes. Yes. She'd say.

11 Start

Chicago streets are lined with abandoned dreams. Old tenements full of new immigrants. Rows of two flats stand dull with porches painted Chicago gray, buildings where wave after wave of Sister Carries dreamed escape from rural gloom. Mansions on Prairie Avenue bought by millionaires to be the seats of dynasties and soon left behind. Factories on the West Side abandoned by hands gone to other, distant tasks. A South Side of Irish ambitions surrendered to blacks. One finds structures proudly built for a present that soon became a forgotten yesterday.

This is that Chicago everyone understands, bone of bone, flesh of flesh. This is the America that dazzled and frightened wave after wave of observers. The place where Tocqueville found men planning stone houses that would shelter their great great grandchildren, then selling them before the roof was finished. The country where Washington Irving writing after the War of 1812 tried to capture Old New York. The country where Henry James poking with his pen around Washington Square after the Civil War tried to capture Old New York. The country where second generation immigrant novelists would find their first generation parents as antique as Romans, where black novelists would find in the move North a feel and distance as strange as a Homeric myth. Here the past has been destroyed so swiftly that it can hardly be recalled, much less understood.

This opportunity to move on into the future has always been our strength. Leaving is the American way of beginning. Now this is changing. The past is increasingly difficult to erase, the

185

future more difficult to run away to. Everyone senses a new day has begun, but ignores this feeling and pretends the clock has not struck midnight.

The past slips steadily away, and the present grows bolder in every act, becomes more difficult to deny. Schemes are floated to avoid the issue. Urban renewal will do what the industrial boom of the nineteenth century once did, build a new Chicago. Gentrification, the return of middle class taxpayers, will revive the spirit of the Gay Nineties. Or perhaps a new industrial park in Lawndale will restore the magic felt on Christmas Day, 1865, when the Union Stockyards opened, or match the surge of energy felt from Cyrus McCormick's reaper works.

The image of the past pulls so strongly that in the Chicago of the late twentieth century disease begins to look like health. Giant schemes to fix errors suddenly are offered as new industries. Slums and traffic snarls become the Big Rock Candy Mountain. The endless woes of disposing of waste on a bog and yet keeping the Lake pure now are seen as opportunities for work and a new era. The deep tunnel of muck and moles that bedevils Andre excites the city's leaders with thoughts of jobs. The project, known as TARP (Tunnel and Reservoir Project), now weighs in at twelve billion dollars.

The meeting is in the Monadnock building on a cold, wet April day, 1978. All the pieces of the puzzle are present, all the slices called micro and macro are embedded in TARP. For that is the problem of the city and the tunnels: resources decline and the price goes up and up to maintain the flow of goods and to expel the flow of wastes. Whether one talks of a greenhouse next to Mike's bar in Pilsen, or Dick on the roof fixing six old apartments, or an industrial park in Lawndale, or purifying the nation's waterways to EPA standards. Or a sewer system. The price and the nature of energy penetrates everything and asks questions of everything. It is in the room at the meeting and in the minds of the humans at the meeting and it is hard to talk because the issue is so simple. The big solutions are impossible and for Americans the little solutions are unthinkable.

The Monadnock marks a fitting place for such a confrontation. After pioneering many features of the modern skyscraper, the Burnham and Root design pulled back from the final element of a steel frame. The Boston capitalists who intuited Form Follows Function in their criticism of ornate urinals and stained glass lost their nerve over the idea of a building held up by nothing more than a lacework of steel. They chose brick. So the Monadnock became in many ways the first of its kind. The future is always hard to believe even when one can touch it in the present.

A federation devoted to saving the Lake hosts the gathering. Michigan laps the shore a few blocks away but no one can see it from the office. The meeting room has no windows. The purr of processed air fills it.

There are a dozen people here, with about a thousand ambitions and cross purposes: a coalition. They are united in their common doubt concerning the deep tunnels. The guardians of the Lakes simply want to protect Lake Michigan, and this is a piece of work. Lake Erie over by Cleveland empties itself and swallows a load of new water in about 30 months. Michigan takes 110 years. Bits of ash and burned bone from the Great Fire in 1871 are just clearing Michigan's system. The PCB dribbling in from the opposite shore has a century of life ahead of it in the flesh of the Coho salmon that draw fishermen to the shore every spring.

Some of the people are organizers from neighborhoods that they do not go home to at night. There is the ex-divinity student. For months and months they have been rubbing up against each other at grant-funded retreats where they wrestle with the future of work and the absence of work. They look over vast districts without jobs and see the carnage of automation everywhere. Economic theory promised that all this would be compensated for by economic growth, but they have scanned the thickets of statistics and found black holes of numbers where hundreds of thousands of Chicagoans have slipped into the limbo of no work or bad work. The newspapers announce that TARP, the deep tunnels, will produce jobs. Sixteen hundred temporary construction jobs. For twelve billion dollars. Not good enough.

The social science professor blew the whistle on the whole matter. In a metropolitan area of five or six million humans, the deep tunnels somehow snuck up on everyone. With billions at stake, they went unnoticed while everyone made merry chasing dollars marked OEO or CETA or VICI, or CLOUT. Now men are two hundred feet below the pavement gouging away. The professor notices. He asked, What is going on there? He says, "Think small."

Then there is the wizard of neighborhood technology who has brought the Whole Earth Catalog to the Windy City. He sparkles as he delivers a paper on local solutions to local excrement. How about holding ponds in the parks? Water storage on the rooftops? Clivius toilets? Egyptian mouth breeders here and there? A wonderland of cheap, labor intensive alternatives to deep tunnels. Everyone says they love the paper. No one believes it. Waves of cholera wash across their faces.

A lawyer from Hyde Park talks water laws. A sanitary engineer explains how the city's sanitation system works and does not work. He sees it as a mechanical system, not a philosophy, and he wants to tinker here and there and not get lost in causes. Finally, a real downtown lawyer in a three-piece suit speaks up. He's just been to the state capitol at Springfield and he reports on what the politicians and bureaucrats think of the deep tunnels. For $50 plus expenses per hour he has explored the secret heart of government, and the heart doubts the future of the deep tunnels. He promises more patrols in the months ahead.

But all the talk and all the reports add up to a blank. The deep tunnels will not work because of design flaws such as storing the shit and urine of millions of people in the aquifer where many of the people get their well water. The deep tunnels spring from a problem in the American mind—the belief that many of the ugly facets of the way Americans produce goods are marginal accidents rather than inherent in the work itself. It is time to face the fact that the dirt is not a by-product but part of the product.

Thus, the federal government has set water standards that cities like Chicago can meet only by ceasing to be cities like Chicago. The twelve billion dollars for the deep tunnels and ancillary features will not make the Chicago River a trout stream but will merely cut the stench. Should the project be finished, no one stone sober thinks it will be a model for all other cities with bad water and fouled sewers. The cost proves the solution has no future. There is no cheap way to clean up the industrial mess of an industrial city. In the past, human beings lived and died with the mess. Now the price of cleaning it up is to increase forever the price of every activity in the city. These escalations in cost are everywhere. Better housing is more expensive housing; better roads are more expensive roads. Better air? Solid gold chimneys would be cheaper than what would have to be done.

Can these costs be avoided? They have to be confronted sooner or later. Pay for better housing or pay for violence and broken lives. Pay decent wages or pay the costs of controlling people who do not get decent wages.

Can these costs be reduced? No. They can only increase because the energy to move things and make things increases in price and because the materials decline in cheap, concentrated forms. In the past thirty years, as the American population has increased 45% energy consumption has risen 250%. Those kinds of numbers slap you in the face everywhere you turn. The oil and the natural gas decline and give out and everything that replaces them is more expensive. Books tumble from the presses, groaning with these facts and figures. Believe them, or wait a few more years and live them. Going to find more oil? Two million wells have been punched in the United States, four times as many as in the rest of the non-communist world combined. This republic is Swiss cheese. Nuclear? Fission reactors are like the deep tunnels—endless structural costs to contain the flows and forces. Fusion? Same time, next century. Solar? Terrific, right up there with $50 oil. Wind? Well, wind.

There's plenty of work to be done in the American city, but the ability to do work cheaply is ending. That is the rub. We still face the unfinished business called decent housing, clean air, clean water, full employment. In the past, no one managed to afford these achievements or allocate money for them when oil cost a buck-and-a-half a barrel, and was plentiful. How are they going to be done now?

That is precisely where the humans in the meeting go vague. Their knives are sharp for the horrors of deep tunnels, but their nerves fail at the prospect of five or six million humans squatting over clivius toilets. Think small, yes, but can they act small? It is the same everywhere. The car is doomed, but everyone drives one. The freeways are the pathways of dinosaurs, but they continue to reach out relentlessly for more earth. Urban renewal? Fiasco. But what else is offered? Big government is bad but no one can conceive of a meeting to criticize big government without a federal grant. Growth must end, but only after the next big project. The future may be inevitable, but for most it is still unthinkable.

So the meeting breaks up that wet April day without con-
clusion, without a coherent response to the deep tunnels. These
meetings will go on until the moment that future knocks down
the door and announces it is here. Most people will continue to
believe that something will turn up, a big, quick, cheap fix for all
that ails the soul and body. The rest will sense their society
moving to an era of fewer goods and less energy, but they will
think of other things for the moment. The refusal to face facts is
a problem in Chicago and on the farm. The future is not bad or
terrifying. It is incomprehensible.

There are several facts that are difficult to accept.

The standard of living declines. As the price of energy rises, as
concentrated resources—trees, iron, phosphate, you name it—
diminish, it takes more energy or money or work to accomplish
the same act, to fabricate the same object. Inflation records this
fact in the money system.

Alternative sources of energy will develop slowly, and they will
never be as cheap as petroleum products. They offer not an
escape from rising energy prices, but only a promise that energy
sources will be available in the future. Americans are not expe-
riencing a transition between cheap oil and cheap something else.
They are entering a future of more expensive something else.
They are entering a future of more expensive sources of energy
and more expensive materials. Any plans that ignore this reality
are doomed, and promises that claim to overcome it are false.

Arguments about cleaning up the air and the water and over-
coming pollution are moot. The population cannot endure the
rising discharges of chemicals and particulates into what they
eat, breathe and drink. The battle about the American landscape
is not about aesthetics or wilderness areas or rare birds and bugs.
It is about the cells in the human body and their ability to with-
stand poisons. It is about the cycles of the sun, water nutrients in

the land, lakes, rivers and streams, and their ability to continue to trap sunlight and produce food in amounts and kinds capable of maintaining human life. So, the arguments about cleaning up our land do not address whether or not the nation is cleansed; they ask whether or not Americans live or die.

Yet, regardless of how expensive energy becomes and how straitened the standard of living becomes, life can be abundant and rich. There will always be Saturday night and Monday morning. The nation enters the future with legacies from the cheap petroleum past that are not dependent upon that past. These include, to name a few, medicines, birth control, electronics, and the enormous amount of information generated by studies done in the age of petroleum. There are many others, but just contraception and antibiotics alone offer significant control over life and death. Talk of going back to a stone age is foolish. People know too much for such a fate to be destiny, unless people by failure of nerve demand such a fate.

The contrast of the Sunbelt with the Frostbelt is increasingly a fraud. The Sunbelt is the last boomtown of the petroleum age, and is tied to cheap petroleum. Its industries and cities are designed and anchored to cheap oil and natural gas. As prices rise and deliveries decline, the sun dims. If tomorrow threatens with dark skies, the worst storm warning is for the southern and western tier of states now explosive with growth. Here, the only significant past is the oil barrel and it has led to the design of transportation and housing and work based on cheap energy. The very locations now blossoming in deserts and fringe areas cannot survive without cheap transportation. The older, declining regions of the north are the product of boats and railroads. These modes of movement have a vital future, as do mass transit systems. Better Chicago than Phoenix in the days and nights ahead. The buildings talk this point. Our new structures rising with glass skins and high rise grandeur are the real jeopardy. They only function if flows of fuel and materials are cheap and plentiful. The old buildings succumbing to the bulldozer's blade are the real resource and the real promise. They were built in an era of smaller flows, the era of the past and again of the future. The Frostbelt is a warehouse of housing stocks and transportation arteries compatible with what is to come. The sooner this is realized, the sooner we can enter the future on a sound footing.

The greatest threat to our society is in our heads. We are still scrambling to avoid the parts of the future that have arrived. We finance automobiles we cannot afford. We build roads we cannot maintain. We scheme mortgages on houses ill-designed for high energy costs, and we locate them in places inaccessible to our work. We continue to move people off the land so that it can be worked by machines, although the power systems behind the machines are in a terminal decline. We must look conditions in the face. Then we can start.

One condition we must face is that we will remain for decades an urban people. We now number hundreds of millions and there is not room for all of us on the land. Our adjustment to higher material and energy costs and to more labor-intensive ways of farming and manufacturing will require several generations. We did not get to State Street in one fell swoop. So let us not talk of the death of cities, unless we mean to talk of our own deaths. For *we are the city,* now, tomorrow, and the days and nights after that.

As city people, let us face our past, not as a failure or success, but realistically. Our cities have been barbarous, and if we choose to tame them it will be a new thing. If neighborhoods are to be stable and nourishing and all the things we claim for them in our folklore, we must change them. People in them must have more power than they have ever been granted in the past, and humans in them must have more commitment to these small areas than they have ever made in the past. The rise of energy costs makes such changes increasingly likely and possible. Our ability to throw away our past, to leave it, to bulldoze it, declines. If we are to make the good life, we must make it where we now stand, not somewhere else. We can no longer postpone the promise of American life until we get to the suburbs or get to California or get to another plateau of the economy. ⟩

⟨ We do it here and we do it now or not at all.

Start.⟩

⟨Our past is one of constant flight from constant presents.⟩ Over the mountains, across the prairie and forests, trekking the Great Plains, wandering in the deserts, onward to the Golden Shore. Problems? We'll solve them next year, next state, next region. Just wait, more growth, and it will all trickle down to wherever you are huddled. Need something? Go west. Need something? Move to town. Need something? Move to the city. Need something? Go West, or go South. Need something? Go to outer space and found a colony. We have been to Vietnam and now we are coming home, like it or not. We now lack the land to go to and the fuel to get us there. We have escaped into a future we must live with.⟩

⟨It is up to us. Do we really believe we fix our crumbling cities by hightailing it to the suburbs?⟩ The Sunbelt? Overseas? Outer space? Do we solve the problem of Pilsen by moving out Mexicans and moving in middle-class Anglos? Do we remedy all our Lawndales with eviction notices? What comes after Houston, Phoenix, and L.A.? Is paradise really hiding in Orange County, or is it simply the making of another yesterday?

Time to belly up to the bar for a stiff drink and a long thought. What we face is freedom from a past that has driven us from pillar to post. As the cheap fire that has driven us becomes too costly to sustain, the problems and the solutions return to the scale of our own bodies. We can see freedom as a threat and insist that all we are about is devouring goods, and when the goods cease, we cease. We can say that the end of the automobile is the end of us, the end of the all-electric home is the end of us. That when they turn off the air conditioner, we go too. Or we can say that we are about freedom and that freedom means using our muscle, that freedom means running our own neighborhoods, that freedom means being in control of our lives and being responsible for our own lives.

We know we have not been this for a long, long time. We have built power systems with coal and oil and broken atoms we cannot comprehend or control. We have made a fetish out of alienation from our own world and a cult out of our loss of control. We have defined ourselves as the people who were not responsible, the people who were victims. As Father Marquette's Immaculate Conception gave way to the canal city and then the railroad city and then the petroleum city, we have defined our courage by our ability to endure forces unleashed upon us. Now we can again put our hands on the levers as power descends to a scale and a place within our reach. We can seize the power or we can deny the new reality and endure failure.

This future like all the others will have no blueprint, just conditions. It will not mean the end of movement and opportunity. It will mean the end of escape.

It will mean freedom.

Freedom.

A strange and terrible beauty.

Start.

196

12 Running Wild

Next to Mike's bar in Pilsen, the greenhouse now leans against the wall, its glass angled for the winter rays. The garden has harvested a crop of tomatoes, tomatillos, chilies, and corn. A fiesta has marked the occasion with a hundred pounds of fiery meat, tortillas and beer. Somebody donated a live lamb and, for a while, it nibbled and browsed the lot of weeds and stubble. A lamb right there on 16th and Halsted, where men fought the battle of the viaduct in 1877, just a couple of blocks from Maxwell Street where the Jews began their wanderings in the new promised land. You can almost toss a rock and hit the old site of Cyrus McCormick's reaper works, and only a couple of blocks away Pope John Paul II paused in Chicago on the steps of the church, the church where the meeting took place with the alderman, and addressed the poor of the city. A goddamn lamb in the shadow of Sears Tower.

It got loose, running down Halsted Street, scampering toward the ruins of Hull House. The guys that hung around the bar saw this lamb bounding down the street and took up pursuit, chasing and driving at it.

The cops came, zoomed in and gave them a ticket, you know. Gave Mike a ticket.

X., MIGUEL   S. HALSTED Sex M Race L
Location of Violation
West ROOSEVELT ROAD
Situated Within The Corporate Limits
Of The City of Chicago.
Aforesaid

Did Then And There Violate ANIMAL AT LARGE (ONE LAMB)   197

So downtown to pay the ticket, what can you do? Walking down State Street, the ticket clutched in your hand. No cars on State Street, they've made it a mall, you know, help business. Look, there in Marshall Field's window, look. A Cadillac Seville in the window. With a dummy in it.